D1318445

Lithography

LITHO GRAPHY

A COMPLETE HANDBOOK OF
MODERN TECHNIQUES OF
LITHOGRAPHY

HENRY CLIFFE

WATSON-GUPTILL PUBLICATIONS
NEW YORK

Acknowledgements

The author would like to thank The Pratt Graphic Art Center, New York for allowing the following plates to be reproduced: 4, 5, 7-12, 27, 29, 33, 34. Also The Bath Academy of Art for the loan of students' work, The Curator of Prints, The Cincinnati Art Museum and The Curator of Prints, British Museum, London

© Henry Cliffe 1965
Published 1965 in London by Studio Vista Limited
Published 1965 in New York by Watson-Guptill Publications
Reprinted 1967
American Edition edited by Federico Castellon
Library of Congress Catalog Card Number 65 – 15948
Set in 12 pt Garamond 1 pt leaded
Made and printed in Great Britain by
Staples Printers Limited, at their Rochester, Kent, establishment

Contents

List of plates

Bibliography

The Art of Lithography by Henry J. Rhodes. Scott Greenwood, London, 1914.

Handbook of Lithography by David Cumming. A. & C. Black, London, 3rd edition, 1932 Macmillan, New York, 1932.

How to Draw and Print Lithographs by Adolf Dehn and Lawrence Barrett. American Artists, New York, 1950.

Rudiments of Lithography by Thomas E. Griffits. Faber & Faber, London, 1956.

Printing and Litho Inks by Herbert Jay Wolfe. MacNair-Dorland, New York, 5th revised edition, 1957.

Printmaking Today by Julius Heller. Henry Holt, New York, 1958 Pitman & Sons, London, 1959.

Printmaking by Gabor Peterdi. Macmillan, New York, 1959.

Autolithography by Henry Trivick. Faber & Faber, London, 1960.

A Handbook of Graphic Reproduction Processes by Felix Brunner. Alec Tiranti, London, 1962 Hastings House, New York, 1962.

About Prints by S. W. Hayter. Oxford University Press, London and New York, 1962.

Offset Lithography by L. E. Lawson. Vista Books, London, 1963.

History of Modern Graphic Art by Wolfe Stubbe. Thames & Hudson, London, 1963.

Artist's Proof. Bi-annual magazine published by The Pratt Graphic Art Center, New York.

I

Approach to lithography

The process of printing called lithography was invented by Aloys Senefelder about the year 1798. Tales relating to the actual discovery are many and romantic, but the facts are uncertain and need not concern us.

The first lithographs were drawn upon a fine-grained limestone called Kelheim stone, found only in one or two quarries in Bavaria. The process became very popular early in the nineteenth century, and many of the great painters and engravers of the time made lithographs, including Goya, Daumier, Bonington, Gavarni, and others; the principal painters of the Impressionist movement also produced lithographs, in both line and tone, in black and white and in colour. The popularity of the process has fluctuated, but it has been much used by artists in this century again – Picasso and Braque among them – and over the last fifty years both painters and sculptors have become more and more interested in making editions of lithographs, and many new and exciting techniques have been developed as a result.

All the earlier lithographs were drawn on stone, but it was only a question of time – in this century – before zinc and aluminium became recognized substitutes for the heavy, cumbersome lithographic limestone; the metal sheets were about ·25 *in* in thickness.

Lithography was popular with commercial printers in the late nineteenth and early twentieth centuries – an important reason being that the number of copies can be almost unlimited. But with stones only flat-bed printing is possible, which is relatively slow, and consequently the medium fell into disrepute among commercial printers. A zinc plate, however, can be fixed round a cylinder so that rotary printing is possible; and so lithography again enjoys commercial popularity.

I propose to deal with lithography only as it affects the artist printer, but there is no doubt that the technical advances that have taken place in the commercial printing world – the advances in the making of inks and the development of other materials – have been of great value to the small studio, and have made lithography both simpler and more exciting.

Lithography differs from the other printing processes in that the impression is taken from a completely flat surface. In relief printing, parts of the surface of the block are cut away and these parts, which do not take the ink, make the white lines and patches in a design. In intaglio printing the opposite is true: metal plates are engraved by one of several processes and the ink is rubbed over the surface and then lightly wiped off so that it remains only in the grooves or scratches on the surface. The fact that the word 'etch' is used for one of the processes in lithography might lead one to suppose that lithography, too, is some form of intaglio process; but it is not. The process is planographic; that is to say, the image forms part of the surface of the plate or stone upon which it is drawn.

Printing from a flat surface is dependent upon the natural aversion of grease for water. The design is drawn on the grained surface of the plate or stone with greasy inks or crayons, and the whole surface is then damped. The grained surface helps to hold the water while the ink repels it. The whole plate or stone is then rolled up with a printing ink which sticks to the greasy drawing, but not to the wet surface of the untouched zinc or stone.

This is the basic principle of lithography, although the actual process of producing prints by this method is a little more complicated, as will be seen.

In lithography it is not necessary to cut or scratch the surface, as it is in etching, woodcutting or engraving, and this is what makes the quality of a lithographic print distinctive. The artist can draw upon the smooth stone or plate naturally and with freedom. This enables him to use any graphic means of expression; the drawing can be linear or in the mass, the image soft or strong and of powerful quality.

If one could compare an oil painting with a symphony – the similar wide ranges of tone and colour which both can encompass – one could reasonably compare a colour lithograph with a trio or quartet. The three or four instruments impose greater restrictions in keeping within their capabilities, and similarly the three or four colours used in a lithograph. The mixing and modulation need particular skill and imagination.

Every print creates some new insight into the medium; every new overprinting of colour must be stored in the mind for future use. Each print is a new experience which may extend the frontiers of the medium. I am always surprised at the result of each new lithograph; something has happened which I never imagined would be possible, and it is the anticipation of this happening, and the excitement of it, which makes lithography the ideal printing medium for the painter. I have found that making a lithograph helps to clarify my ideas in painting and, of course, that painting helps in the conception of a lithograph.

Lithography is a process capable of great refinement and subtlety, of rich exuberance of colour; it is capable of rendering large and powerful images, of delicate drawing, of a wide and exciting range of textures – the possibilities are virtually unlimited. But in order to exploit the medium to the full one must understand and adapt oneself to the techniques. A lithograph is the result of a fine balance between the designer and the printer – who may well be one and the same person.

A lithographer should be aware of the *quality* of his prints; he must have a sensitivity to the craft itself. It is the means whereby he realizes his ideas; but he must also be aware that the medium itself will have a hand in shaping them.

It is true that lithography can merely be a means of reproducing drawings and designs in some quantity, but if this is the artist's attitude towards it, the results will be without vitality. To be successful in lithography, design must be spontaneous and yet within the limits of the medium, and in order to achieve this one must understand and be able to handle with confidence the various processes used in the production of a lithograph.

2

Zinc and aluminium plates; lithographic stones

Lithographic prints can be made using zinc or aluminium plates, or stone.

Aluminium is the most limiting material of the three as it is delicate, and alterations and deletions are more difficult. It does not really give the same scope for the wide variety of effects that are possible with zinc and stone.

Aluminium and zinc plates rely upon a mechanically produced granular surface to retain dampness – an essential factor in lithography – while the granular surface on stone is produced manually by the artist.

Personally I prefer zinc plates. All my editions have been produced from these, and with care and common sense results equal to those obtained from lithographic stones are possible, without any of the weight-lifting stones involve.

Plates come already grained from a printers' supplier and they can be worked upon straight away. When they are to be re-used they must be sent away to be regrained (at a cost of about 3s to 8s, according to the size of the plate). Where facilities for regraining are not easily available, the artist buys new plates. There is, of course, a limit to the number of times a plate can be regrained: a dozen to fourteen times as a rule. Finally they can be given in part exchange for new plates. A zinc plate 24 *in* × 16 *in* costs approximately 16s in Great Britain and $3·75 in the United States, and a 32 *in* × 22 *in* plate somewhere around 30s (around $6·50 in US).

When lithographic stone was superseded commercially by zinc and aluminium plates, a large number of stones became available for schools of art and for artist printers. Naturally many stones were broken up or used for other purposes as well, but a useful residue remains. The price of a good lithographic stone varies from 3d to 9d a pound weight in Great Britain (a stone 12 *in* × 16 *in* × 3 *in* costs $15 in the United States), and generally speaking the larger the stone the more the cost per pound.

There are some advantages in using stone: it can be used many times and re-surfaced at very little cost; it is probably easier to make deletions; scratching can be employed as part of the drawing technique; and stone is naturally absorbent and very little trouble should be experienced in keeping it damp. On the other hand, I have found that when working on stones with students, the cleaning and graining of the stones creates a bottleneck in the printing programme. The larger stones are very heavy and usually beyond the power of women students to lift single-handed, and there is obviously a danger factor with these heavy stones. Owing to their size there may be a storage problem, also, in any workroom where space is limited. Finally, to print a lithograph of any size, say about 20 in × 28 in, stones of at least 32 in × 24 in are necessary, and that is working with a small outside margin. For this size the stone has to be no less than 5 in thick. Imagine the weight of a stone of that size, and the trouble of moving it around, and this for each colour of the lithograph. A zinc lithographic plate of the same dimensions can be picked up with two fingers and stored in the same space as a sheet of thin card.

Lithography was invented using stone, and stone was used extensively for well over a hundred years before metal plates came into use. Consequently its use has become hallowed by tradition. But, after all, in any craft the materials and techniques are used only to produce the effects desired, and if metal plates can give all the variations that are possible on stone, using the same basic principle of the antipathy of grease and water, then I think that the convenience of plates far outweighs the advantages of the more cumbersome material. One can, in fact, obtain all the effects possible on stone with a zinc plate – with the exception of scratching, and there are ways around this. The careful chalk (or crayon) drawing of the past has in any case been succeeded by a greater variety of texture and effect, and by using zinc plates it is possible to produce the finest and most subtle graduations of tone, and to maintain them throughout the printing of an edition.

3

Making a lithograph

It would be a pity if a student were to become lost among all the possibilities of the medium at the outset, and so I propose, as an introduction to the subject, to explain simply how I myself go about making a three-colour lithograph, before going through each of the processes in more detail in the following chapters.

I start thinking in the direction of a lithograph, perhaps after looking through a number of working drawings and paintings in gouache, perhaps after working on a group of paintings. A particular image or a certain colour scheme may be the starting point, but, and this is important, the lithograph must always be worked within the range of two, three or at the most four coloured lithographic plates – which will, of course, produce a wider range of colours by over-printing. It is, of course, possible to use more than four colour plates, but I have found from experience that if more than four, or at the most five, plates are used in large areas of the drawing, the print tends finally to have an unpleasant shine. I do several colour drafts, bearing in mind the limitations of over-printing, before settling on one particular idea.

When I have made up my mind as to the general form of the litho-graph, I then consider which colours would be the best to get the effect I want, and the order in which they should be printed. Any colours I decide to use can be transparent or opaque, and the order in which they are printed will be a major factor in the final appearance of the lithograph. For example, if the first colour is black, any colour printed on top will change it: if I print an opaque, medium blue on the black the result will be – black, white paper, dark blue-grey where the blue overprints the black, and blue printed directly on the white paper. Now if this is the result of printing one colour on black, imagine the result of printing yet a third colour – say, a transparent violet, warm in colour – over the other two. The violet where it over-prints the black makes the black appear darker, more velvety; on the blue it makes a muted blue-violet; on the white paper it prints as violet, and where the three colours meet it makes another variation of blue-violet. Therefore three colour plates give seven colours and white – and this is a fairly conservative colour range. No colours here are widely dissimilar (see illustration, plate 14). One can, of course, make very striking differences by using colours such as turquoise over yellow, or transparent blue over brown. Both these combinations produce very strong third colours; turquoise over yellow gives a brilliant green, and blue over brown gives black.

Every time I print a lithograph I keep a few prints of each colour on its own, as well as some prints of two colours together. I can then try out different overprintings on them to see what the results will be, and keep these experiments as records for future lithographs. Only experience of overprinting in colour can give any true assurance of the appearance of the final print. I work to the plan that the darkest colour is printed first, especially if it is black. When black is printed last it gives only black, but, as I have said, if it is printed first there are many more variations.

When I have decided upon the main image of the lithograph, I choose the colour which is to play the main part. On this occasion, using three colours, I am supposing that the main one is to be black.

I take a clean, sensitive plate – by sensitive I mean that it will hold grease – and decide on the proportions of the design within it. I tend to work within the proportions of the plate being used, usually 32 $in \times$ 22 in, leaving about $1\frac{1}{2}$ – 2 in all around the drawn image. This ensures that the final print will have clean edges.

Preparing to draw the first plate is like learning a part in a play: one uses the script at first, but it has to be memorized for the actual performance. I find that if a tracing is made from a sketch and carefully followed, there is a tendency to woodenness and a lack of vitality. It is much better to draw the first plate with freedom. Drawing on a plate has a feeling and quality quite unlike anything else, and this itself suggests many variations on the original idea. It is wiser, therefore, to accept this rather than try to stick to a rigid conception. I think it is the accidental qualities and variations which give lithography part of its unmistakable quality. I always think of the first plate as the bones of a print: not merely a drawing to be enhanced with colour, but something which gives the lithograph its particular strength and flexibility.

When drawing the first plate – in this case the black plate – it is as well to bear in mind that apart from the linear drawing and the solid areas, beautiful qualities can be obtained by leaving out shapes and areas within the solids, with the intention of overprinting these areas with one of the succeeding colours. The quality of a colour will be very different when surrounded by another colour from what it is when printed alone on white paper. It is always my aim to make use of all the possibilities and variations of each colour overprinted.

It is important to be sure that the drawing is on the plate the right way round – the image in reverse for direct press printing, the right way round for offset – for, if the work is to be printed from a direct machine the printed image will be the reverse of the plate, but if an offset press is being used, the plate and print read the same. Reversal must therefore be allowed for when printing direct, and this may be done either by drawing the image on the first plate in reverse, or by tracing it on to the plate in reverse from a drawing.

When I have drawn the first plate, I must then process it. This means strengthening the greasy image that is to take the ink; it is a chemical process and is described in Chapter 6.

I print about six copies of the black plate – enough copies to enable me, after trials, to have one print to my satisfaction – on good, but not necessarily expensive, white cartridge paper. Bockingford Hot Pressed (available in UK and US) is a good paper for this purpose (see page 61). Newsprint can be used when proofing a colour; it is quite inexpensive, but an edition of an artist's lithograph should be of the highest quality possible and a print on newsprint will not give a fair idea of the appearance of the finished print. If a plate is not behaving in a favourable way, certainly it would be useful to have a very cheap paper for taking many proofs, but the final proofs need to be on a paper good enough to give one a satisfactory idea of the appearance of the edition itself.

Now I take a sheet of good tracing paper or a sheet of frosted acetate and trace off from the black print anything which will help in drawing the second plate. Usually I trace the whole drawing so that the same tracing can be used for the third plate also.

The tracing is now laid on the fresh plate, over a piece of tracing-down paper, making sure that the plate is large enough to leave an equal space all round the image to be traced. Nothing is more irritating than to have the image crooked on the plate, or to have uneven margins round it.

The tracing-down paper is a thin, but strong, white paper which has had one side, the face, impregnated with jeweller's rouge; it is laid face down on the plate. The paper can be bought already prepared, or rouge (or sanguine) can be rubbed all over a piece of plain paper with a cotton-wool (absorbent cotton) pad. Alternatively, the violet dye powder used by lithographers for making offsets on machine plates can be used, though it has the drawback that should your hand rest on the tracing for any length of time, the powder tends to blur.

It is important to be sure that the tracing is on the plate the right way round. When printing from a direct press the printed image will be the reverse of that drawn on the plate. All tracings from this first *plate* must, of course, be lifted and laid down on subsequent plates the same way up, but if the tracing is taken from a *print* of plate one, then the tracing must be reversed before being laid on plate two, etc.

This procedure will not be necessary when printing from an offset press. The plate and the printed image are the same. The tracing must not be reversed, therefore, when laid on either plate or print.

The tracing and tracing-down paper are held in place on the plate with lead weights of about $\frac{3}{4}lb$, which prevent any possibility of the tracing moving. Instructions for making them are given on page 88.

After tracing down the important parts of the drawing from the first plate, I draw the second plate, process it and prove it – that is, print the second colour on the first to find out if it is satisfactory – and then do likewise with the third plate.

The system of printing the second and third plates is exactly the same as that used for the first one, except that the second colour must be registered accurately on the first, and the third colour on the first and second (see page 64). This is no problem when printing with an offset machine, as it is more or less automatic, but as an aid to registering when using a direct machine I use the following system.

After the drawing of the first plate has been completed, I put a small dot on both ends of the plate, about $\frac{3}{8}$ *in* away from the boundary. These dots are then marked on the tracing, with the image, and thus are transferred to the second and third plates. Some people prefer to draw a small cross, but I think that these show too much on the final print and spoil its appearance when it is framed. The marks are put on the shorter sides of the plate because, with a direct press, the bedstone and plate enter the press shorter side first. The bedstone is a lithographic stone which has been ground and polished to an accurate thickness and smooth surface. Cast iron or mild steel bed-plates can be purchased in various sizes, but in my opinion a lithographic stone is better. (See page 64 for the actual registering of the colour plates during printing.) When the three plates have been drawn and processed, and any alterations and additions have been made (page 51), the lithograph is ready for printing.

Summary

1 Decide upon the size of plate, the number of colours in the lithograph and the order in which they are to be printed.
2 Draw the first plate. Make register marks, if printing on a direct press, and process the plate.
3 Print about six black copies of the plate.
4 Take a sheet of tracing paper and trace off what is necessary for the second plate.
5 Place tracing-down paper face down on the second plate.
6 Lay tracing squarely on top of the tracing-down paper, leaving a good margin all round the image, and making sure that it is in reverse if printing is to be on a direct press. Hold firmly in place with lead weights.
7 Trace off drawing on to second plate. Draw plate and process.
8 Trace, draw and process third plate.

Materials

Tracing paper, or film.
Tracing-down paper, or thin white paper, jeweller's rouge and cotton-wool (absorbent cotton) pad.
White Bockingford paper, or similar.
Drawing inks, chalks (crayons), etc. (page 22)
Lead weights.

4

Preparing zinc, aluminium and stone for drawing

All zinc and aluminium plates and stones must be grained before use, and for this an abrasive – flint sand, carborundum or garnet powder – is used. Plates, however, are obtained from the suppliers already grained, whereas stones have to be grained by hand.

Preparing zinc and aluminium plates

The grain on zinc or aluminium is usually made by putting the plate into a large tray fixed to an electrically driven eccentric shaft. The plate is then covered with an abrasive, usually carborundum powder, wetted and the whole plate covered with marbles up to an inch in diameter and made of glass, porcelain or wood. The tray is moved and the balls rotate over the abrasive on the plate. But the more technical details of this process need not worry us, as it is unlikely that artists or students will grain their own plates.

The grain varies in texture: fine, medium, poster or coarse, depending upon the job it is to be used for. Aluminium plates can take a finer grain than zinc plates. For myself, I always use a medium-fine grain.

Zinc and aluminium plates should always be kept flat while being worked or in storage. If plates have been in store for some time, or have been left uncovered, they cannot be worked on until they have been rinsed all over with dilute sensitizer. In the case of zinc this is nitric acid and alum, and with aluminium plates it is a weak solution of oxalic acid (page 53). It should not be necessary to do this when first working on new plates.

Preparing a lithographic stone

Lithographic stones vary in their hardness, yellow ones being the softest and grey the hardest. Both are used by lithographers today.

Preparation of a lithographic stone requires patience and energy. The old work or drawing on it must first be removed from the surface, and for this purpose a piece of coarse grit stone (or another lithographic stone) is useful. A good piece of sandstone with a flat surface can usually be bought or begged from a stonemason's yard. Alternatively a hand-levigator can be used. The levigator is a heavy cast-iron disc, usually about 12 – 14 *in* in diameter, and about 2 *in* thick. It

FIG 1 Levigator

has 2 *in* wide holes through it to prevent it from sticking, and a wooden or metal handle set eccentrically (see figure 1).

Sharp flint sand or carborundum grit, varying from very fine, powder-like dust to coarse-grained, are used as abrasives. These abrasives are numbered 60-hole, 80-hole and 120-hole, etc., meaning that the powders have been passed through sieves with a given number of holes to the square inch. I personally have found 80-hole and 120-hole abrasives the most useful.

The lithographic stone that is to be cleaned is placed in a sink – the bigger the better as no one likes hitting his knuckles. A stand made from 4 *in* × 2 *in* teak or another hardwood, placed in the sink, is useful for keeping the stone clear of the dirt and used abrasive at the bottom. It can be constructed by fixing battens (boards) across two side pieces.

Now begins the hard work, and skill as much as muscle is needed to clean the stone well.

First wet the stone all over. A short length of hose fixed to the tap is useful as it enables the flow of water to be directed at will. When the stone is wet, sprinkle a handful of coarse abrasive over it: 80-hole. Place the grit stone or levigator at the near left-hand corner of the litho stone and, using a circular motion, work in an even and systematic manner all over the stone, and back again until all the old drawing is removed. The levigator spins round the handle, and it may require a little practice to work it, but you should soon be able to clean off a stone quickly with one. From time to time the stone must be washed thoroughly and fresh abrasive grit used, as after grinding for a while the abrasive loses its cutting qualities. When the drawing has been removed the stone should look perfectly clean and feel roughly textured.

The stone then receives its final graining. I find that 120-hole graining sand gives a surface which is capable of giving good, flat, solid areas of drawing as well as fine and sensitive chalk drawing or wash.

The procedure is: wash the stone thoroughly, removing all coarse grit from the surface. While thoroughly wet, distribute a handful of 120-hole sand over the stone. Take another lithographic stone, smaller in area than the surface being grained and, using the same circular rhythm, work over the whole surface of the stone about twelve or fifteen times. The smaller of the two stones should always over-reach the edges of the larger or a hollow may be worn in the centre of the surface. It is absolutely essential, too, that a strict system of rotation is used in graining. If the surface of the stone is uneven the printed surface will also be uneven, and this means trouble and wasted time ahead. If there is any doubt about the flatness of the grained stone, take a true-edged metal ruler and, placing it on different positions on the stone, look for gaps between the metal and the litho stone. If a strict system of graining is followed there will be no hollows or bumps, and this check should not really be necessary.

When the stone has been grained it must be rinsed thoroughly until every particle of sand has been washed off. By using the side of the hand to remove the grit and some of the water, you can see if the grained surface is even or if it needs yet more graining. If there are still some hollows or bumps, graining must begin all over again and continue until a really flat surface is achieved.

Graining a stone correctly is fairly hard work, and graining three or four is a good test of anyone's interest in lithography. If after this you are still enthusiastic you are off to a good start.

5

Drawing and drawing mediums

All drawing mediums for lithography must have a basis of grease, and all may be used on both metal plates and stones with the exception of tools used for scratching, which can only be used on lithographic stones.

It is important to have a flat, clear space for drawing plates, so that all the equipment can be close at hand.

Drawing on zinc or aluminium

Any means of drawing can be used: chalks (crayons), brushed ink, bamboo pens, etc. I have sometimes wetted the plate and drawn direct with a stick of litho drawing ink (tusche). See figure 2 for this use of wash technique on stone.

Scratching with a knife or needle is not practicable on zinc or

FIG 2 Work with diluted ink on wet stone

aluminium, so instead I use an ordinary pen, or a sharpened stick with a saturated solution of caustic potash. It is quite simple to draw with this liquid, which should be left for a few minutes after application and then rinsed off under the tap, taking care that it does not come into contact with any other part of the work, or with hands or clothing. Caustic potash is highly corrosive and therefore potentially dangerous.

There is always the thrill of discovering some new way of putting a drawing on the plate, by printing-down textures, or by using soft greasy crayons, lipstick or soap, and so on.

Always rest your hand on a pad of paper when drawing on the plate. Finger marks and smudges are a nuisance and take time to remove.

It is not recommended that deletions to the original drawing be made until the plate has been processed and charged with ink (page 51).

Drawing on stone

Chalk, brush or any mixture of techniques can be used. For bolder lines you can draw with a quill or bamboo. It is possible, too, to use a wash technique on the stone, and this is done by using a very diluted solution of lithographic ink (called tusche in US). I usually wet the stone and then carefully work with diluted ink (see figure 2).

It is possible to get white lines or marks by taking a sharp penknife blade or other sharp-edged tool and scratching or scraping into the solidly drawn areas of ink or chalk.

Drawing mediums

INKS Lithographic ink, or tusche, comes in the form of a stick 1 *in* × 4 *in* × $\frac{1}{4}$ *in*, in black and it looks rather like a stick of toffee. It is an emulsified grease which readily mixes with water. Tusche may also be bought in liquid form. I prefer stick tusche but when large areas of solid drawing are required I make a liquid from small pieces of the stick dissolved in distilled water.

The method of preparing it is simple. Take a clean dry saucer or shallow bowl and rub the stick around it until the ink starts to form slight uneven bumps. Now add a few drops of clean water and rub it round the bowl until the ink has all dissolved. If it seems very thick add a few more drops of water; but remember, it is easier to dilute the ink than it is to strengthen it again, though this can be done by rubbing down more ink in another dry saucer and adding the weak ink to it. The mixed ink should work easily in a brush and appear fairly black in colour; too weak an ink will not give solid areas in the drawing.

Methods The ink (tusche) can be used in many ways: with brushes of different kinds – sable, hoghair (called bristles in US), and so on – with bamboo pens or with ordinary pens; you can dip a small piece

FIG 3 Drawing with a brush, wet and dry

FIG 4 A piece of writing paper was screwed into a ball. It was then unscrewed, rolled up with black ink and pressed on to a sensitive plate

FIG 5 The same technique was used but the crumpled paper was pressed into gum etch. The negative print is not wholly successful because the paper does not hold gum as well as ink

FIG 6a Corrugated paper rolled up with ink and pressed down on to a sensitive zinc litho plate

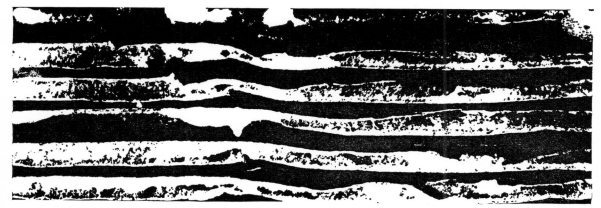

FIG 6b Corrugated paper pressed into gum etch solution. Both images work reasonably well

of sponge in the ink and draw with it. Different textures can be made by putting ink on linen canvas or rough papers and printing these down on to the plate or stone (see plates 1, 2, figures 4, 5, 6a, 6b, 7a, 7b). Another variation can be made by drawing with clean water on the plate and drawing straight in that with the stick of ink. This gives a broad, powerful quality to the drawing (see figure 3).

WASHES It is quite easy to use washes of ink on lithographic plates once a sense of control has been felt. I use two methods of putting washes on a plate: either I draw first with clean water and then introduce a small amount of liquid ink into the water, or I mix a wash first – liquid drawing ink mixed with more water – in a saucer beforehand. These two methods can be varied or combined. The important thing is not to make the wash too strong or it will print solid black (or whatever the colour being printed), while if the ink is too weak it will not print at all. Only trial and error will give skill in using washes.

CHALKS Lithographic chalks (crayons) are greasy chalks about 2 *in* long and $\frac{1}{4}$ *in* thick. They are black like the drawing inks (tusche) and are made in different degrees of hardness: number 0 is the softest chalk, and the degrees of hardness rise to 5 and 6. The earliest lithographs were drawn entirely with chalks, and the artists were extremely

FIG 7a Strips of torn paper rolled up with ink and pressed on to a litho plate

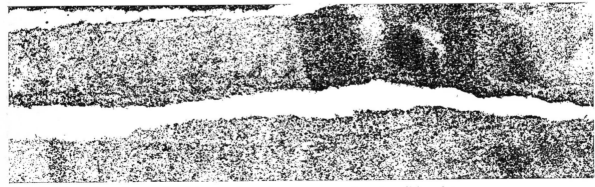

FIG 7b The strips of paper for this negative print were pressed on to a litho plate. The negative print is the less sensitive because the paper absorbed quite a lot of gum and so made the negative image much whiter

skilful at rendering a multitude of tones on one stone using this means alone. The effect produced, however, is that of a chalk drawing, and it is likely that we should regard the use of chalks alone as unnecessarily limiting today when so many freer and richer effects can be obtained by combining them with lithographic inks. Chalks are, in fact, particularly useful in conjunction with washes. By using them as textures over large, flat areas the print is given interest and sparkle (plate 3).

OTHER MEDIUMS Obviously every artist lithographer will find personal ways of using any medium. I have recently used some of the Japanese oil pastels; they are smooth and velvety in texture and make a rich quality on the plate. Experimentally I have also used lipstick and hard soap to produce different qualities in the drawing; both these are interesting, but the effects obtained by them lack sharpness. It would be interesting to work with oil pastel and a solvent such as benzine or lighter fuel. Gasoline might also be used, but kerosene, because of its drying qualities, might present difficulties in use. The particles of grease would be in temporary suspension and when the solvent evaporated might produce interesting washes, as when particles of drawing ink, suspended and distributed in clean water, settle on the plate as the water dries. Figures 8a, 8b show the difference between a positive and a negative image, and how some surfaces lend themselves to transferring more than others (figures 9a, 9b).

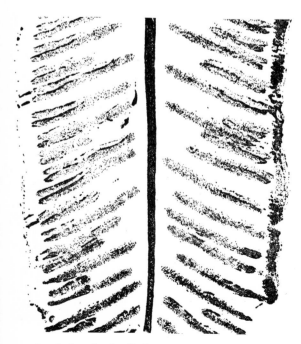

FIG 8a A fern leaf rolled up with ink and printed on to the plate

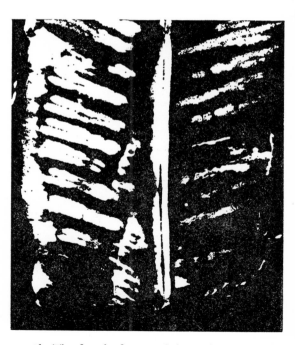

FIG 8b The fern leaf pressed into the gum does not give such a sensitive result

Materials used for drawing on zinc or aluminium plates

Litho chalk (crayon)   Bamboo pens
Litho ink (tusche)   Dip pen
Japanese oil pastels   Sharpened stick
Potassium hydroxide   Abrasive etch stick
   (or preparations such   Pumice powder
   as 'Erasol,' etc.)

Erasing solutions such as caustic potash, or the proprietary 'Erasol' can be dangerous if they come into contact with the artist's skin or eyes and should be used with care. Potassium hydroxide will not harm zinc plates but on no account must it be used on aluminium plates.

Materials used for drawing on stone

The same materials as for metal plates may all be used, and a knife for scratching.

FIG 9a A hand print was made by placing a hand on the inking slab and then on the litho plate

FIG 9b A similar procedure but this time the hand was pressed down on a thin layer of gum etch and then on to the plate.
  Both negative and positive work well because a hand is soft and has a sensitive surface

26

6

Processing zinc, aluminium and stone

After drawing, the plate or stone must be processed in order to reinforce the greasy image that is going to take the printing ink. There are several stages in this processing, and they involve the use of chemicals and other substances; the three most important are:

Etches

The various chemical substances used for putting a grease-resisting layer on the undrawn areas. It is not, as in the more usual sense, a process involving corrosive action such as that on copper used in etching.

Gum

Gum solution is used both as a protective layer on a drawn plate or stone and as a vehicle for the etching substances.

Washout

Washout solution is an asphaltum solution which reinforces the greasy image while turpentine is removing the colouring matter from the drawing.

Etches

I have advocated the use of ready-mixed proprietary etch solutions in this book in order to show that many traditional and complicated practices are no longer necessary. However, some enquiring person may like to mix an etch solution. The chemicals can be mixed with either warm water or thin gum solution.

The following formula is suitable for use on zinc plates:

Ammonium nitrate	1 *oz*
Ammonium bi-phosphate	1 *oz*
Warm water or gum solution	20 *oz*

The etch for aluminium plates is:

Phosphoric acid 20%	1 *oz*
Gum solution	10 *oz*

The use of these etches will be described under the heading *Gum Arabic*

Method. I do not advise the use of chromic acid as it is extremely dangerous and no better in action that the formula already given.

So many etches must be prepared by the printer by mixing chemicals with either gum or water, that this could mean pitfalls for the beginner unaccustomed to dealing with printing chemicals. I have used several types of etch in the past but the easiest by far is a gum called 'A Gum Z'. It is a synthetic gum containing the necessary chemicals to de-sensitize the plate and make it moisture retaining. As it is a synthetic gum there is no tendency for it to go sour or mouldy, and if it is kept in a bottle with the screw top in place it will keep indefinitely. (I cannot give any information concerning its formula as it is a pro-prietary brand of etch.) Two other etches which I have used with success are 'Victory Etch', which can be obtained from most printers' suppliers and 'Zetch', which is made by Algraphy Limited. Both these etches are most efficient, but are not gum etches; because of this more time is needed to process the plate. American equivalents are available from the Rembrandt Graphic Arts Co.

Gum arabic solution

Gum arabic is bought from printers' suppliers either in the raw state, that is in the actual lumps which were exuded from the acacia tree, or in powder form.

In the case of the raw gum arabic the solution is made by soaking the lumps in cold water. The solution should be made in the same way as a simple sugar and water syrup. When the gum has completely dissolved it should be strained through a piece of muslin in order to get rid of any pieces of vegetable matter, seeds or particles of bark.

For the sake of speed and utility, the gum is best bought in the powder form, because when the powdered gum is added to the water, the gum powder will dissolve much more quickly than if the raw lumps of gum were used. *Two* parts of powdered gum should be used to *three* parts of clean water. The gum arabic solution should be of the same consistency as hot treacle (molasses), plenty of body but not too viscous.

Gum arabic has an unfortunate habit of going sour if kept for any length of time. The deterioration can be retarded by adding one or two drops of carbolic acid, but this must be done with care, as too much carbolic acid would ruin any work to which the gum solution was applied.

Processing a zinc or aluminium plate

When the drawing on the plate has been completed, it must be given a protective layer. There are two ways of doing this: with a gum etch or with plain gum arabic. The gum solution is used to de-sensitize, which means to render the plate non-sensitive to grease, i.e., to protect from finger marks, etc., or from oxidization.

When a plate has been printed it should always be covered with gum to protect it until it is next required.

GUM ETCH METHOD   I use the solution already mentioned called
A Gum Z. This method of etching a zinc plate is the quickest, and
not only has it halved the time normally taken by other methods, but
the plates tend to print better too.

A Gum Z is used as follows: dust lightly all over the drawn plate
with french chalk; then with a soft sponge cover the whole plate with
A Gum Z etch solution, wiping it thin with a rag and the side of the
hand, until only a very thin layer remains covering the whole plate.
Fan the plate dry.

Next wash out the drawing with turpentine and washout solution;
the turpentine and washout solution remove the colouring matter of
the chalk and ink used in the drawing, leaving only the grease on
the plate. Remove all excess turpentine and washout solution,
and wipe the plate dry.

Place the plate in the sink and wash it thoroughly with clean water.
When all excess water has been removed and the plate is evenly damp
all over, it can be placed on the press, rolled up with printing ink and
printed.

This is the simplest and most effective way of processing a plate
that I have used. If any difficulties are encountered when printing the
plate, it is advisable to gum it up with A Gum Z before examining
any filling-in of the drawing, or any piece of the work which is not
receiving ink. It should be a first rule with all beginners in lithography
that *whenever difficulties are met with in printing, the plate should be gummed
up at once;* then the trouble can be found without fear of further
damage.

GUM ARABIC METHOD   A second method of processing a zinc
plate is one using a liquid etch that is not mixed with gum. There are
several proprietary brands sold. I have experience of one called
'Victory Etch' which is sold in Britain by most litho printing supply
stores.

Here is the procedure for using Victory Etch on zinc or aluminium
plates:

When the plate has been drawn it should be fanned dry and lightly
dusted all over with french chalk. This not only makes sure that all
the ink is dry but prevents any smudging. French chalk also acts as a
protection to the drawing.

Cover the whole plate with a layer of clean, fresh gum arabic
solution of the consistency of thin treacle (molasses). Wipe the plate
with a rag and the side of the hand until only a thin film of gum
remains. Fan the plate dry and place it on a flat surface where there is
no danger of water being splashed on it, as this would of course
dissolve the gum and expose the plate.

Pour on a pool of pure turpentine (the amount naturally depends
upon the size of the plate) and a slightly smaller pool of liquid
asphaltum or washout solution. With a woollen rag gently but firmly

rub away the drawing until only a faint ghost remains. Now wipe off all the excess turpentine mixture with an absorbent rag until the plate is dry and smooth.

Place the plate in the sink and wash it thoroughly all over with clean water. If the process has been successful the layer of gum will wash away, taking all excess turpentine and washout with it and leaving the drawing clean and sharp.

Make sure that you remove all excess water, especially from the back of the plate, before carrying it to the place where it is to be rolled up with ink, or the press or the rolling-up bench will become messy.

Damp the plate evenly all over with clean water; it should be matt damp, not wet.

The drawing must now be inked. This is in order to make a powdered mixture of french chalk and rosin stick to the drawing and thus protect it during the second etch.

Using a roller charged with the ink you intend to use, roll the plate until all the drawing has received ink to your satisfaction, being careful not to go on rolling so long that the plate becomes dry. This is a common fault with beginners, who are so absorbed in watching the plate take the ink that they forget the plate is drying out. Should you make this mistake, however, immediately damp the plate all over, then pass the roller lightly but quickly over the work and it will pull off any unwanted ink. (For inking and rolling-up see page 62.)

When the plate has been inked to your satisfaction, dust the drawn parts all over with a mixture of powdered rosin and french chalk (slightly more rosin than chalk) or, if you prefer, first dust some rosin and then some chalk across the plate. Tap the edge of the plate on the table and the excess powder will come off.

Put the plate in the sink and cover it all over with Victory Etch. By moving the plate gently from side to side the etch can be made to flow all over the surface; alternatively a soft sponge can be used. The etch should be left on the plate for about four minutes, or a little longer. (It should be possible to pour the etch back into the jar, using the corner of the plate as a spout or guide.)

Wash the plate thoroughly with clean water; once more remember to remove all excess water from both back and front of the plate. Using clean blotting paper, reduce the water on the printing surface of the plate to a slight dampness and, using a soft sponge, cover it with clean gum arabic. Wipe it thin all over the surface and fan the plate dry.

The procedure is now the same as at the beginning of the process, with turpentine and washout solution. Then wash away the layer of french chalk, rosin and ink on the drawing, wipe the plate clean with an absorbent dry rag and wash it with water in the sink until only the drawing remains. Remove all excess water once more, especially from the back of the plate. Put the plate on the bed of the press, and with a clean rag make the surface evenly matt damp. The time has now come to roll up the drawing with ink (see page 62) and to take the first print.

The process I have just explained is obviously longer than the gum etch method, but as an alternative it is equally successful.

Summary of series of operations for processing a zinc plate

METHOD USING A GUM Z

1 Protect drawing with gum etch, or plain gum arabic. Wipe it thin and fan the plate dry.
2 Wash out drawing with turpentine and washout solution. Remove excess and wipe plate dry.
3 Wash plate thoroughly with clean water, remove excess until evenly damp all over.
4 Roll up with ink.

METHOD USING GUM ARABIC

1 Fan finished drawing dry and lightly dust with french chalk.
2 Cover plate with gum arabic solution. Wipe with a rag, fan plate dry and place on a flat surface.
3 Pour pool of turpentine and another of washout solution on plate. Rub away drawing with woollen rag. Wipe off excess moisture with absorbent rag until plate is dry.
4 Place in the sink and wash thoroughly with clean water.
5 Remove all excess water from both sides of plate, and carry to rolling-up bench.
6 Damp plate all over.
7 Roll up plate with ink. Do not let it become dry.
8 Dust all drawn parts of the plate with powdered rosin and french chalk. Remove excess powder.
9 Place plate in the sink and cover with Victory Etch. Leave for four minutes or longer. Remove excess etch.
10 Wash plate thoroughly with clean water and remove excess water from both sides of it. Blot plate till only slightly damp, and cover with gum arabic solution. Wipe thin and fan dry.
11 Wash away drawing with turpentine and washout solution. Wipe plate clean with a dry rag and wash it in the sink. Remove excess moisture and place on the press. Damp the surface of the plate.

Materials used for etching zinc or aluminium plates

A Gum Z *or* Victory Etch *or* Zetch (best kept in a jar – say a 2 *lb* jam jar – to avoid wastage) and gum arabic
French chalk
Powdered rosin (this is ordinary cheap rosin or collophany used by dancers for their shoes)
Pure turpentine
Liquid asphaltum or washout solution
Sponge   Dry rags   Woollen rags   Blotting paper   Fan

When the drawing has been completed on the stone it must be etched. The materials needed are gum arabic and nitric acid. The chemical process has never been satisfactorily defined, but it is known that the two substances combine to make a grease repellent film on the non-printing areas of the stone.

The nitric acid is extremely corrosive and is naturally dangerous. A small bottle of concentrated nitric acid should last a long time.

Making the etch is a simple operation, but one which needs some practice. It is made in the following way:

Pour gum solution sufficient to cover the stone liberally – into a flat dish, or a soup plate. Into the gum thoroughly mix two or three drops of nitric acid. Now take a little of the mixture on the tip of a finger and put it on the edge of the stone well away from the drawing. If it effervesces violently it is too strong and more gum must be added until an extremely weak reaction only is obtained. Ideally the etch should have a delayed action; that is, the weak action of the etch on the stone should only begin slightly after it has been applied.

Having satisfied yourself that the etch is of the right strength, take a 4 *in* wide soft brush with a flat edge, or a soft turkey sponge (natural sponge) of about the same size, and cover the stone all over with the etch. This must be done systematically so that no part of the stone is covered twice; 'float' the etch all over the surface; *on no account* rub it. The stone should now be left until the following day to dry and to give the etch time to work on the stone.

The next stage is to place the stone in the sink and to remove gently all traces of the dried gum etch with clean water and a sponge (the industrial rectangular 'Spontex' sponges are ideal for this). When all the dried etch has been removed the stone should be dried until it is only slightly damp all over. Then take a sponge dipped in gum arabic solution and run it all over the stone. (You need a separate sponge for the gum as it must be quite free of acid.) Then, using a clean rag and the side of the hand, wipe away all surplus gum, leaving a thin even film on the stone. Dry it by fanning (see page 87).

When the gummed stone is perfectly dry, and this is important, place it on the work bench away from the sink. Get two pieces of clean, soft rag, large enough to fill the hand, a bottle of pure turpentine and a bottle of liquid asphaltum – or washout solution. Pour on to the drawn and evenly gummed stone a pool of turpentine about 3 *in* in diameter (or more for a very large stone). Into this pool pour about half as much washout solution. Take one of the pieces of rag and rub over the drawing until it seems to disappear. All the black chalk (crayon) and ink (tusche) must go; it is always an alarming experience to see all your precious drawing disappear, but if you have gummed it up evenly and thoroughly nothing will go wrong. When all the

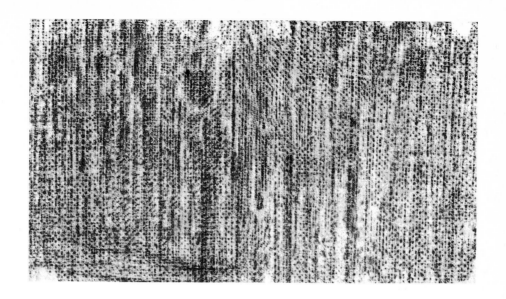

1 and 2 Printed-down texture from linen and wood

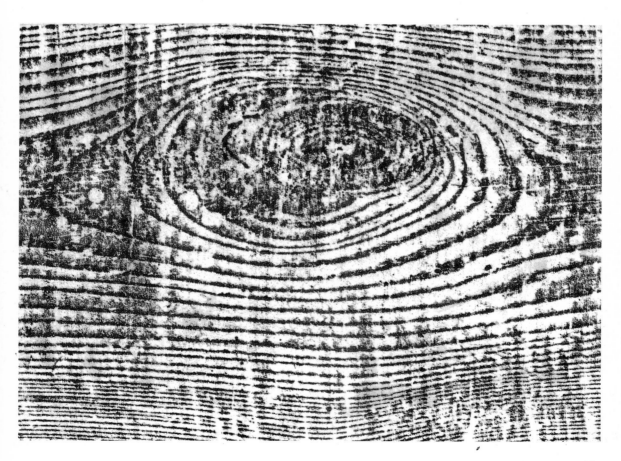

33

3 Drawing with chalk

4 *October* 1960 by Andrew Stasik, lithograph.
Achenbach Foundation of Graphic Arts, San Francisco

Betty 10/20

Arnold Singer

5 *Betty* by Arnold Singer, lithograph, black and white

6 *Composition* 1960 by John Gridley, lithograph, red and purple printed on black to give a variety of reds, browns and blacks

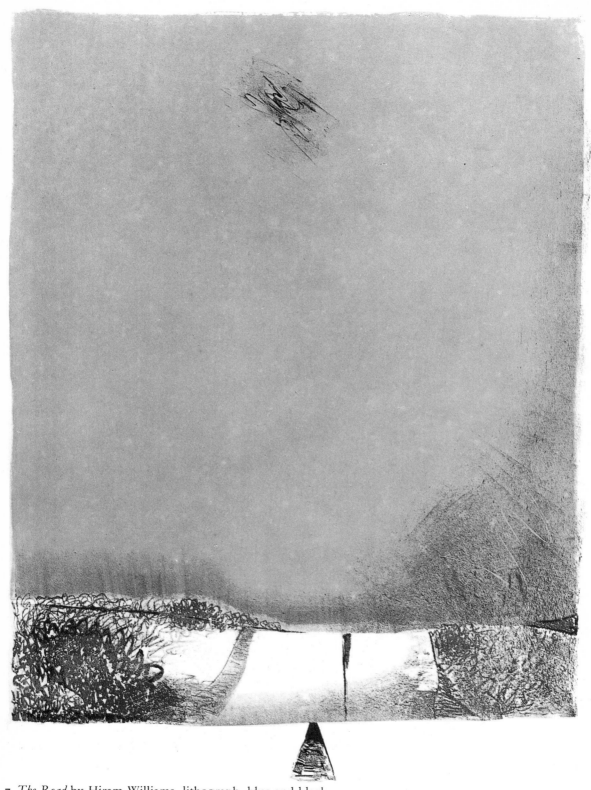

7 *The Road* by Hiram Williams, lithograph, blue and black

8 *Spring Rite* by Andrew Stasik, lithograph (with serigraphy), blue, black, sienna and ochre

9 *Self-portrait* by Robert Andrew Parker, lithograph, black and white

10 *Mundigrama* by Michael Ponce de Leon, lithograph, blue and red

115/200   Haitian Caryatids   Adolf Dehn

11 *Haitian Caryatids* 1952 by Adolf Dehn, colour lithograph.
Cincinnati Art Museum (Gift of Albert P. Strietmann)

12 Untitled lithograph by Tad Lapinski, maroon, grey and blue

13 Lithograph by Goya

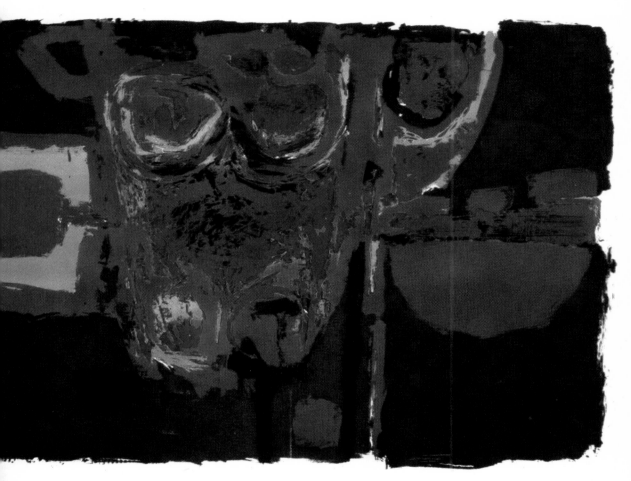

14 *Brooklyn* 1962 by Henry Cliffe, lithograph, black, purple and pale blue

15 *Les Beaux Jours de la Vie* 1886 by Daumier, drawn in lithographic crayon on stone

16 *Dancer* by Toulouse-Lautrec, drawn in lithographic crayon on stone

17 Lithograph by Matisse

18 *Dancer* by Toulouse-Lautrec, in brush splatter and chalk

19 *Argyl Castle* 1866 by Bonnington, lithograph in chalk on stone

13/50

20 *Nude* by Picasso

21 Lithograph by Géricault

22 *Nude* by Fantin-Latour

drawing has been seemingly removed, take the second rag and wipe away all excess turpentine and washout until the stone is evenly wiped and dry.

The next stage in the process is one of the most exciting, for at this moment all the work of drawing and etching on the stone will be brought together, and you may wonder whether this is really going to result in a lithograph. Providing that all stages of the work have been carried out carefully, however, you should be rewarded when you have placed the stone in the sink and are washing it with clean water by seeing your drawing develop in a pale brown, as the gum arabic dissolves and takes the film of washout solution with it. This is the greasy image which will receive the printing ink and repel the water.

Take a clean, damp sponge and a clean piece of damp cotton rag or mutton cloth (or sponge) and remove all excess water from the stone, making sure that its surface is *damp all over*, but not wet. Take the ink roller and a little ink (black ink is best as it enables you to see the sharpness and tone of your work) and roll up the image on the stone (see page 62). Roll quickly and without too much pressure until the drawn image looks like the original drawing. Should it become dry and you continue to roll up, the stone will take ink all over it. If this should happen, immediately redamp the stone and pass the roller over it a few times, using slight pressure. You will then find that the roller pulls off all the unwanted ink and scum.

The stone is now ready to receive its second etch. It is necessary to roll up the stone with ink and to etch a second time to reinforce the ink-resisting layer on the undrawn parts of the stone.

First dust the dry stone all over the drawing with a mixture of french chalk and powdered rosin. This mixture is an acid resist; it sticks to the ink which you have rolled on to the image and will protect it during the second etch. Before this takes place, however, any accidental marks or smudges round the edges of the work may be taken off, either with the edge of a penknife or with a stick of 'Water of Ayre' stone (UK name) – a grey, natural abrasive also known as 'snakestone' (US name). Damp the area of the unwanted mark and rub it away with the snakestone, keeping the area constantly damp.

The second etch differs from the first in that the acid is dispersed in clean water and not gum arabic – a few drops of nitric acid to a cupful of clean water. When the stone has been well dusted with the french chalk and rosin mixture, carry it to the sink for applying the etch. The second etch can be slightly stronger than the first one and the acid and water mixture may be rinsed off after a matter of seconds. Three or four seconds should be time enough. After the stone has been rinsed clean it is partially dried; the surface should remain just damp as this facilitates the distribution of the thin layer of gum arabic that you must now apply. Care must be taken once more that the layer of gum is wiped thinly with the clean gum rag and the side of the hand. Dry the gummed surface with the fan.

The stone is now washed out with pure turpentine and washout solution and wiped clean.

The final stage is to wash the stone in the sink with clean water, put it on the press and remove any surplus water. When the stone is the correct dampness roll up the image until there is enough ink to make an impression. (For rolling up and printing see page 62.)

Summary of method

1 Etch the drawn stone with gum arabic and nitric acid (a very weak solution). Leave overnight or for some length of time.
2 Wash off gum etch and re-gum stone with pure gum arabic solution. Dry thoroughly.
3 Wash out drawing with pure turpentine and washout solution. Wipe stone clean and dry.
4 Wash stone under a clean water-tap. Make sure all traces of washout solution and turpentine are removed.
5 Damp and roll up stone until it looks like the original drawing.
6 Dust stone with french chalk and powdered rosin.
7 Apply water and acid etch. Rinse off.
8 Re-gum stone with clean gum arabic. Wipe thin. Dry.
9 Repeat washing-out operation with turpentine and washout solution. Wipe thin and clean.
10 Wash stone under running water.
11 Put stone on press, damp evenly and roll up the work.

Materials needed for etching stones

Gum arabic
Nitric acid
French chalk and powdered rosin
Pure turpentine
Washout solution
Sponges – 4 *in* brush
Clean rags – cotton rags for gum and water; fine woollen rags are best for turpentine and washout solution, although cotton rags, being absorbent, will wipe a stone cleaner.
Glass or stone jar to hold the gum (with a wide enough neck to enable you to get your hand in it – a large pickle jar will do).
Flat dish or soup plate for etch
Fan

7

Alterations to the image

There is usually some point during the making of a lithograph when one wishes to make alterations to the drawn image. It is possible to make these at any time during the process, but I have always found it best to make additions or deletions after the plate has been processed and rolled up with printing ink, as it is then less easy to damage the other parts of the drawing on the plate.

In order to remove work from the plate or stone, before re-drawing, a chemical solution has to be used. The chemicals involved are not complex or expensive, but their misuse can ruin a plate and so great care is needed when applying them.

Most of the sensitizing solutions used are made of a mixture of dilute nitric acid and alum. The amount and strength of the acid are extremely important, for if the acid is too strong the grain of the plate will be removed and the plate spoiled. Different printers' supply firms make their own brands of sensitizing solution, which are usually of similar composition. The strength may vary, but it is normally necessary to dilute it before use. (One or two brand names are mentioned on page 53 with particulars about their use on zinc plates.)

Sometimes it is necessary to use abrasive methods to get rid of unwanted work on zinc or aluminium plates. Abrasive sticks, or etch sticks as they are sometimes called, are to be had from most printers' suppliers and are usually made with a combination of pumice powder and a de-sensitizing compound. If an abrasive stick is used, it is important to handle it with a light and circular motion. This is because the grain of a plate is put on with a circular motion, and should one rub indiscriminately the grain will be removed and the area of the plate so treated will take up ink from the roller, and so spoil the plate.

A wise habit is to apply etch whenever you disturb or make bare the surface of a metal plate, whether zinc or aluminium.

The method used for making alterations on stone, it will be seen, is rather different.

Deletion of drawing on zinc plates
Dust a large area around the part to be taken out with french chalk. Gum up the area with either clean gum arabic or gum etch (A Gum Z).

Dry the gum layer.

Take a sharpened stick or, if the deletion is a fine one, an ordinary dip pen. Take a little concentrated potassium hydroxide solution (sold under various proprietary names) on the stick or pen and gently remove the unwanted parts of the drawing. I use a caustic potash solution called 'Erasol', made by Aligraphy Ltd (see page 26). The US equivalent is called zinc eraser.

Leave the caustic potash solution on the plate for about five or six minutes. If there are several places to be dealt with, do not attempt to remove the solution until all the parts are deleted, or the caustic solution may find its way over a part of the drawing where it is not wanted.

Sometimes you may wish to make lines that will print white on the black drawing, and the caustic solution will do this. These lines can be drawn in with either the stick or the pen (see figure 10).

When all the desired parts have been deleted, take the plate to the sink and quickly rinse away all the caustic solution. It may be necessary to loosen some parts of the unwanted drawing with the finger or, if it is stubborn, with an abrasive etch stick or a little pumice powder on a sharpened piece of wood, using some gentle rubbing.

FIG 10 Lines made with caustic potash on brush and ink stick drawing

Whenever additions have to be made to a plate, it is best to wash the *whole* plate thoroughly with cold, clean water before the actual re-sensitizing begins. The reason for this is that should only a part of the plate be washed before re-sensitizing there is a danger of some gum etch running on to other parts of the plate and de-sensitizing them again; so it is best to make a clean start and be sure this cannot happen.

To *de-sensitize* a plate means rendering the surface incapable of receiving more drawing, i.e. by covering the plate with a layer of gum arabic or gum etch.

To *sensitize* a plate, wash it under a cold running tap thoroughly. For zinc plates go over the areas to be sensitized with a solution made from

Alum	2 *oz*
Nitric Acid	½ *oz*
Water	80 *oz*

For aluminium plates

1 part of saturated solution of oxalic acid to 25 parts of water.

Wash off the sensitizing solution under a cold running tap. Dry the plate thoroughly. It is now ready to receive more work.

When the whole plate has been washed, the sensitizing solution is applied to the areas where it is intended to add new work, preferably with clean cotton-wool (absorbent cotton). The solution I use is called 'C' solution and is made by Algraphy Ltd, but there are others which can be easily purchased, such as 'Prepasol,' made by Hunter Penrose. American equivalents are available from the Rembrandt Graphic Arts Co. The manufacturers give precise instructions as to how the solution must be diluted; usually it is one part solution to three parts water.

I find it is best to sensitize an area larger than that required, as one can never be certain what changes need to be made to the drawing until one has started work on it.

The solution will have a corrosive action on the zinc plate, so it must be applied quickly and immediately washed off with clean water under a running tap.

The plate should be dried by fanning, or with an electric dryer. Then you can add the work required.

If the additions are to be fine or accurate, use the lithographic drawing ink (tusche) or chalk (crayon) as you did when the plate was originally drawn. If the additions are to be the filling in of spare or thinly drawn areas, or small spots or marks in the solid areas, it is only necessary to take some ink from the inking slab and dab it in the areas with a finger.

When the new work has been added, it is necessary to go over the sensitized areas with gum etch to make sure that no scum or dirt collects on the plate. If the work has been added with litho drawing ink, the plate must be gummed up all over and the work washed out with turpentine and washout. If on the other hand it was added with printing ink, it is only necessary to damp the plate and carry on printing.

Deletion of drawing on aluminium plates

Aluminium plates are more delicate than zinc ones and more care is therefore necessary when erasing, making corrections or adding work. I have found that it is only possible to remove *areas* of drawing on aluminium plates and that it is very difficult to make white lines or textures on the plates. The best method, I find, is this:

First clean off unwanted work with either benzine, lighter-fuel or home dry-cleaning fluid – carbon tetrachloride. Use cotton-wool and repeat the operation two or three times to make sure that the greasy image has been removed from the plate. If using an abrasive stick it is always advisable to go over the area afterwards with A Gum Z or with a weak solution of phosphoric acid and gum; this will de-sensitize the plate. (To make the solution, add 1 *oz* of 20% phosphoric acid to 10 *oz* of gum.)

If no other work has to be added, go over the erased area with A Gum Z (or gum etch solution), leaving it on for a few minutes. This de-sensitizes the area. Wash off the gum etch and carry on printing.

It may be necessary to repeat the A Gum Z treatment while printing an edition as the erased work does sometimes reappear.

Additional drawing on aluminium plates

To sensitize an aluminium plate, first wash the plate thoroughly with cold, clean water and then use a solution of one part oxalic acid and twenty-five parts water. Go over the area which is to be sensitized with this solution and wash off immediately. It is always wiser to use a solution that is on the weak side than one that is too strong. Dry the plate. New work can be added immediately.

Deletion of drawing on stone

If at any time dirty marks appear on the drawn stone during the first rolling up, or during the actual printing, it is necessary, and not difficult, to remove them.

If no more work is to be added to the stone after cleaning it is an easy matter to take the side of a penknife and scrape off the marks or unwanted drawing. An alternative way is to use a snakestone slip. Always keep the stone damp when removing marks, as this prevents any more dirt from sticking to it. If more work is to be added after the deletions have been made, then use the following method.

With a saturated solution of caustic potash, or a proprietary erasing solution such as Erasol (see page 52), carefully and lightly rub the unwanted marks with a sharpened stick dipped in the solution. For a very small area a mapping pen may be more suitable than the sharpened stick. If the area involved is very small, the stone should be gummed and fanned dry before attempting to remove the dirt or unwanted drawing; this will prevent the caustic spreading to other areas.

After the work has been removed with the caustic solution, wash all the stone with clean, cold water and rub the deleted areas with the tip of a finger to make sure dirt or unwanted drawing has completely gone.

Remove as much water as possible with clean blotting paper.

Additional drawing on stone

After washing the stone thoroughly with clean water and removing all traces of gum arabic, the areas to receive new drawing must be re-sensitized. Go over them with cotton-wool dipped in a weak solution of either citric or acetic acid, leave it for two or three seconds and then remove the weak acid by rinsing the stone with clean water. Dry the stone with clean blotting paper. When it is really dry the work can be added.

After all additions have been made, the stone must be gummed up completely. Dry it, and go through the process of washing out with turpentine and asphaltum solution (see page 32) before starting to print again.

8

Presses

There are two types of press available: the old-fashioned direct press and the offset proofing press. Both may be hand-operated or motorized, but I will discuss only the hand-operated presses as they are more suitable for the artist lithographer. It is best to use a direct press for printing on stone because, in using an offset press, it is necessary to remove the metal bed and put the lithographic stone in its place; and the stone must be the same size as the metal bed or it will damage the offset cylinder. This means a fair amount of heavy manual work every time one wishes to change from plate to stone, as well as time spent making the extremely fine adjustments needed between the stone and the rubber covered cylinder.

Direct press

The old direct press is constructed so that the pressure from the central screw is brought to bear on the stone in a sliding fashion. This central screw is fixed on to a slotted metal bar. Into this bar is fixed the scraper – a piece of hardwood, boxwood, ash or beech. Along the bottom of the scraper a strip of $\frac{1}{4}$ *in* thick leather is fixed to it by means of screws or large-headed nails at either end. It is this leather-covered wood bar which actually presses on to the tympan and so puts pressure on the stone or plate. To bring the stone or plate into contact with the scraper, a cross bar with oval lugs at either end raises and lowers a metal roller. This roller comes into contact with the movable press bed – a wooden bed with metal slides which moves backwards and forwards in side rails which are part of the press framework – and when the handle of the press is turned the friction made between the roller and the bed enables the press bed to be turned through (see figure 11).

With metal plates, a lithographic stone is often used in the press bed in order to help bring the plate to the correct height.

The printing paper is laid on the stone or plate, resting on the bed of the press, and is covered with layers of soft paper (sugar paper, cartridge, inexpensive drawing paper or newsprint) which should be slightly larger than the printing paper. These layers break the pressure and help distribute it evenly over the print. Then I like to lay a sheet of ply rubber on top of the layers of paper in order to give still more pliability when pressure is applied, but this is not essential.

The tympan – usually a sheet of greased zinc or brass – is then placed on top. (Sometimes it is made of sheet-leather, but this type is expensive. Because of its softness, however, it allows the pressure exerted to bring the printing paper into even closer contact with the stone.) The tympan is greased to make its passage through the press easier.

When adjusting the pressure on a direct hand press, a good rule is to raise the bed by applying the pressure lever, and screw on the pressure until the scraper is in contact with the tympan. Then release the pressure and give the regulating screw about three turns. The pressure should be correct when the pressure lever re-engages.

These simple presses are easy to use and to maintain, and although rather difficult to find are still obtainable. Sometimes a small family printing firm will sell one when they are modernizing their works. They are of various sizes and are almost indestructible. All that is needed to keep them in good order is oil on the working parts and some stiff grease on the metal or leather tympan.

Offset proofing presses

I cannot hope to describe all the various types of presses that come within this description, but the principle is simple.

Within the metal frame, which is supported on four stout metal legs, are two flat beds. The plate bed is made of cast metal and is adjustable for height and forward and backward movement. The other bed, of ply rubber, is where the printing paper is fixed in position. Down the length of the press on both sides are two toothed rails and, running parallel and outside them, two plain rails which can be raised and lowered. The most important part of the press is a precision-made metal cylinder, usually about 1 *ft* 3 *in* in diameter. It has cogs which run round its circumference at either end and rest on the toothed rails on the press frame. The cylinder is covered with a precision-made ply-rubber blanket, stretched over its circumference. The cylinder runs on the toothed track when the press is in gear and printing is taking place; when the press is not in gear the cylinder rides on the plain rails, bringing it clear of the beds.

To use the press, the printing plate is fixed on the metal bed. Usually a layer of water will hold it in place by means of suction. The plate is then damped and rolled up with ink, the press put in gear and the rubber covered cylinder rolled over the plate. An impression is taken on the cylinder. This impression is in reverse; the cylinder is pushed further on over the printing paper on its ply-rubber covered bed, and the impression is thus transferred to the paper. The impression has been offset from the cylinder to the paper so that the impression on the paper itself will be the right way round.

These presses are expensive and are usually beyond the reach of individual artist printers.

The press with which I am most familiar is made by George Mann and Co. Ltd and prints double crown size (20 *in* × 30 *in*). I use imperial size 22 *in* × 30 *in* paper for printing, to make sure that the actual paper edges are inside the plate edges, thus ensuring that any scum or dirt which might collect round the plate does not come on to the actual printed surface. The complete press weighs about a ton and a quarter.

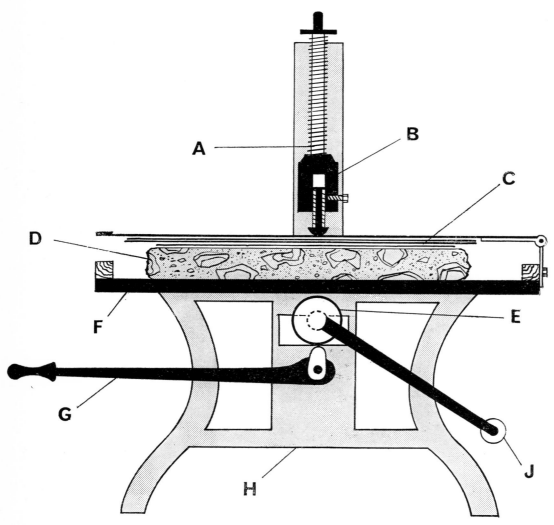

FIG 11 Key to diagram of hand proofing press, showing the method of adjusting and application of pressure.

A Vertical screw which raises and lowers the wooden scraper bar with leather cover B.

C Zinc or aluminium plate with the printing paper and backing papers in place, all resting on lithographic stone D.

E Metal roller which acts as a friction clutch which is in contact with the press bed F.

The pressure is applied by pushing down the lever G; this works an eccentric lug H which brings the roller E in contact with the press bed F. The bed is turned through by using the handle J.

9

Inks and papers

A whole book could be written on the different ink mixtures and additives used in lithography, but in order not to confuse the reader I will refer only to those which I have personally used and can recommend.

Printing inks

Almost all makers of printing inks make lithographic printing inks. As very little direct printing is done today on a commercial scale, inks are not often required for this particular purpose, but, generally speaking, I have found printers' lithographic offset inks are very good and will do very well. Any good manufacturer will give you advice on problems relating to ink or ink mediums, and will even make up special inks for you. They have large research departments and from them you can get expert opinions on such things as light fastness, tinting and consistency of inks. But experience gained by personal experiment is the most important factor in mixing inks.

It is possible to have inks specially made for hand printing, but I find that trade products are generally suitable. It is true that one can only understand various mixtures by using them over a fairly long period of time, and every lithograph has its own problems; for example, a plate which has large areas of solid work on it will require a much softer ink than a plate which has a crisp drawing or texture, and when a plate has a combination of different types of drawing a happy medium must be found which will take care of both.

Mixing inks

The amount of ink to be mixed naturally depends on the size of the plate to be printed, the area of work on the plate and the number of prints in the edition. It is wisest, however, to mix rather more ink than is likely to be needed, rather than have to stop halfway through printing to mix some more. It might be difficult to mix exactly the same colour a second time, and this could mean that the whole edition would be spoiled.

First it is necessary to decide whether the ink is to be transparent or opaque; some inks are naturally transparent. The appearance of the finished print depends on the way it is mixed.

For an example, let us suppose that a medium strong blue which is both cool and opaque is desired for printing on a 32 *in* × 22 *in* plate with a fair amount of drawing on it.

One heaped dessertspoonful of tinting medium is added to about three-quarters of the quantity of flake white printing ink. Tinting medium is a fairly stiff ink made by grinding various substances into varnish, and it has body but no colour.

These substances will be fairly thick, so petroleum jelly or vaseline is added: the amount that could be heaped on a shilling (or a US quarter). Mixed thoroughly, this gives the ink the right consistency. The ink should be kept in a neat piece on the mixing slab, for it is wasteful if the ink spreads all over the stone. A smooth lithographic stone makes an excellent inking slab, and the ink is best mixed on it with a palette knife or paint scraper (figure 12).

Into the mixture of tinting medium, flake white ink and vaseline, a little of the concentrated blue ink is added, perhaps 'mono fast blue', and mixed thoroughly with the palette knife.

A little ink is taken on a finger end and dabbed thoroughly on a piece of white paper. This gives an idea of how strong the ink will look. Gradually more blue is added until the correct strength of colour is obtained.

When a transparent ink is required, no white is added to the mixture, but the same cautious procedure of adding colour gradually should be observed. It is easier to add a little more colour than it is to add all the previous ingredients to make the ink lighter again.

When all the ingredients have been thoroughly mixed it is advisable to add a few drops of paraffin (kerosene) to reduce the ink to a working consistency. It should not, however, be too soft; a firm buttery consistency is correct and will enable it to be absorbed into the paper and not make it lie on the surface. Ink that lies on the surface dries with a shine.

Basic lithographic inks

Press black	Flake white
Light yellow lake	Chrome yellow light
Deep yellow lake	Vermilionette
Crimson or satin red	Ultramarine blue
Mono fast blue	Turquoise blue
Superfine art green (like viridian)	Deep tan brown

These inks should cover most printing jobs, though more individual colours, like magenta or purple, could also be included. To begin with it is wise to order 1 *lb* of each colour, with 2 *lb* each of black, white and tinting medium. Colour names will vary in the United States but equivalent hues are available.

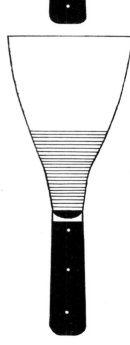

FIG 12 Palette knife for mixing ink. Push knife for removing ink from slab, etc.

Papers

One of the major factors involved in printing a lithograph is, naturally, the choice of paper. Ideally a paper should be reasonably smooth and fairly absorbent. These two qualities are essential to produce fully inked and evenly printed solid areas, crisp detail and correct drying of the ink without shine.

For trial proofs or students' prints, where expense is important, I use smooth or hot-pressed Bockingford cartridge paper, about 100 *lb* weight, or Basingwerk at about 50 *lb* weight. The Bockingford costs about 1*s* 6*d* a sheet and is made by Barcham Green Ltd. Ordinary drawing cartridge paper can be used, but when more than two colours are to be superimposed it is not very satisfactory owing to its inability to absorb much printing ink. Thick imitation Japanese paper will do, but this is not cheap. For producing an edition of really good prints I have found from experience that Crisbrook smooth 100 *lb* weight is an excellent paper. It is hand made and has all the qualities required; it has a wonderfully rich feel and adds much to the quality of the print, which is important. This paper is also made by Barcham Green Ltd and costs about 3*s* a sheet, which makes printing an edition of fifty quite expensive, so there must be no mistakes. These papers or their equivalents are available in the United States from Andrews/Nelson/Whitehead, Inc.

Some authorities on hand printing advise that the paper should be damped. I have never done this and have not found it necessary with plates, although it would be useful when printing large flat areas from stone. Some of the more expensive Japanese papers are excellent for lithographic hand printing. There are many types, white or cream, and some with subtle mixtures of straw in them. These are not for every lithograph but can be used to good effect where richness of quality is desired. Many other papers can also be used effectively, and quite surprising results can come from using papers experimentally.

It is usual practice to have paper with at least two uncut edges when printing an edition. Crisbrook has four uncut edges and this is considered by collectors to give an added quality to a hand produced print.

10

Rolling up

When the metal plate or stone is ready for printing it is carried to the press and placed in position on the bed of the press. It must then be rolled up with printing ink for taking the first proofs.

It is important that the ink is spread evenly over the surface of the drawing to be printed, which means that the ink must be transferred from the inking slab to the roller and from the roller to the plate in a thin even film.

To do this, take some ink already mixed to the right consistency on the end of a palette knife and gently run two or three parallel strips of this ink on to the roller. Roll the roller away from you along the inking slab two or three times. This distributes the ink on the slab. Finally, roll the roller quickly backwards and forwards on the slab to get a good, thin, even distribution of ink (figure 13).

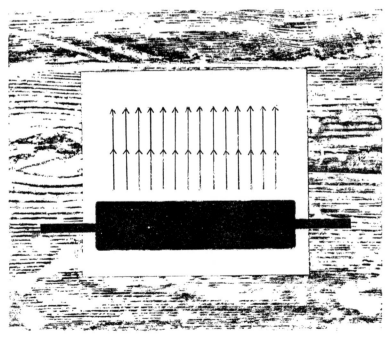

FIG 13 Movement and direction of roller when inking up an inking slab

A good way to tell whether there is too much ink on the roller is by the sound made as it passes over the slab. If it is correctly inked it should make a hissing noise, but if there is too much ink, or the ink is too stiff, it will make more of a crackling sound.

The actual rolling of ink on the drawn litho plate or stone needs great care. My experience as a teacher has shown that this operation is the one thing a student always wants to do for himself, but if care is not taken there will be marks on the plate, lines where there should not be and ink in the wrong places generally.

After the plate has been dampened all over, take the roller and run it quickly backwards and forwards over the inking slab; this removes any lines of ink which may have collected while the roller has been standing on the inked slab. Failure to carry out this operation may result in lines being made all over the plate, especially if there are solid areas of drawing. After making sure there are no lines on the roller, pass it quickly and with moderate pressure over the drawn image and then, if there are large and solid areas of drawing, roll again at right-angles to this. Never go right over the actual edge of the plate or stone or this will again result in lines being made on the drawing; ink will also be left on the edge of the plate where it touches the press bed and will result in coloured lines on the white paper around the printed image which will, of course, spoil any print intended for exhibition or sale.

One or two trial prints will soon show whether enough ink has been applied to the plate; and after two or three prints have been taken it will be possible to tell whether the ink itself is of the right strength. If the colour is too pale it should only be necessary to add a little more concentrated ink. To do this, take the ink off the rolling slab and put it in with the supply of ink on the mixing slab, add the necessary colour and mix again. This ensures that all the ink to be used is correctly mixed. Now take another print from the plate *without* rolling it up first, so as to ensure that all the over-pale ink has been removed; any remaining on the plate or stone may otherwise dilute the colour of the next print you take.

It should now be possible to go right ahead and print all the copies you require (see page 81).

If you are working alone it is almost impossible to keep your fingers completely clean. It is therefore best to use two pieces of folded paper – paper fingers – for placing the paper on the press, removing them after the print has been made. This prevents dirty finger-marks appearing on the edge of the prints.

You may wish, when the trial proofs are examined, to add or take out some drawing on the plate or stone. The various operations needed to do this on zinc, aluminium or stone are described on pages 51 ff. You then take the plate or stone back to the press, roll up again, take trial prints and proceed to print all the copies of the first colour.

The plate or stone must be evenly damped all over and rolled up before each successive print is taken, and each colour of the edition must be hung up on the rack to dry as it is printed.

II

Printing

Registering colours

DIRECT PRESS If a print is being produced on a manually operated direct press, it is necessary to register the paper for the second and further colours in the following way:

Take two needles and push the eye of each into two pieces of ⅜ *in* dowel rod about 3 *in* long (figure 14). This will make the needles into efficient tools for registering the various colours in the lithograph. When the first colour has dried sufficiently push the needles through the two dots or the centres of the crosses which have been marked at either end of the first colour print (see page 17), making the holes just large enough for the pins to slip easily in and out. Turn the print over, so that the image is face downwards, push the pins through the holes from the back of the paper and, holding the wooden handles with thumb and forefinger, place the second finger under the print so that you can hold and control not only the needles but also the print. Place the points of the needles on both dots of the second plate, making sure that it is the right way round for printing. Keep the print fairly taut so that it does not touch the plate prematurely and, when you are certain the needle points are exactly on the register dots, let the print slide down the needles to the correct position on the plate or stone. The same method of fitting is used for each successive colour.

OFFSET PRESS When registering work on the hand offset press it is important that one print should be taken to make sure how the work is fitting. Should any alterations be necessary this is done by adjusting the side and/or end lays. On the press there are screw-held stops which make sure that every sheet goes down on the printing bed in exactly the same position as the preceding copy.

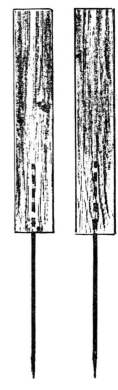

FIG 14 Needles

The rate of drying of each set of prints depends on the colour being used, and this must be taken into consideration before printing the next colour. It takes some experience to know exactly when a colour is dry enough for the next one to be printed on it. Black usually takes two days in a moderate temperature to become sufficiently dry for the next colour to be superimposed. If an attempt is made to print too soon, the pressure of the printing press will transfer some of the wet ink from the paper on to the second plate and this

23 Mann double-crown hand-operated offset proofing press

24 Hand-operated direct proofing press

25 Rack for drying prints

26 Bench section divided for inks, etc.

27 *The Wave* by Shegeru Izumi, lithograph, pale blue and cobalt blue

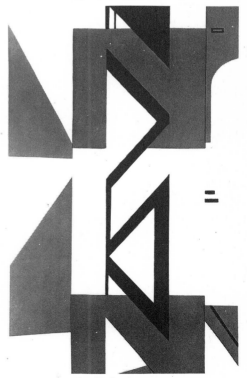

28 *Third Avenue Elevated* 1952 (no. 4) by Ralston Crawford, colour lithograph. Cincinnati Art Museum (Anonymous Gift)

29 *Landscape – Summer* by Andrew Stasik, lithograph (with serigraphy), black, green and ochre

30 *Thy Almighty Word Leapt down from Heaven* by Frank Kacmarcik, colour
lithograph. Cincinnati Art Museum (Mr and Mrs Ross W. Sloniker Collection
of Twentieth-Century Biblical and Religious Prints)

31 *Spanish Fishing Boats* 1954 by John Eaves, drawn with ink and chalk, printed in grey, blue and black. This is a very good example of white being used as a colour

32 *Knight of the Sad Countenance* 1952 by Leon Goldin, colour lithograph.
Cincinnati Art Museum

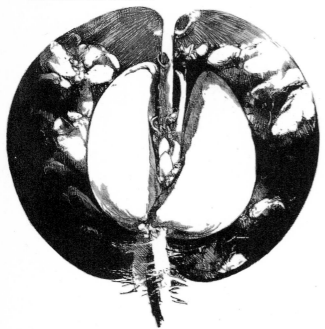

33 *From a Seed* by Lucy Durand Sikes, lithograph, black and white

34 *Summer Horizons* by Michael Ponce de Leon, lithograph, green, blue, red, yellow and black

35 *Space with Beacons* 1949-50 by Robert J. Else, colour lithograph

36 *Owl* 1955 by Jack Smith, drawn with lithographic chalk, the background filled in with ink to give greater vitality to the image

37 *Stonehenge* 1960 by Henry Cliffe, drawn with ink (tusche), some diluted. The white texture was made by drawing with caustic potash and a pen

38 Black and white lithograph 1963 by Henry Cliffe. Some white shapes were taken out by using lighter fuel and then applying gum etch (A Gum Z)

39 Lithograph by third year student at Bath Academy of Art, drawn direct using ink (tusche) and lithographic chalk, printed in black ▶

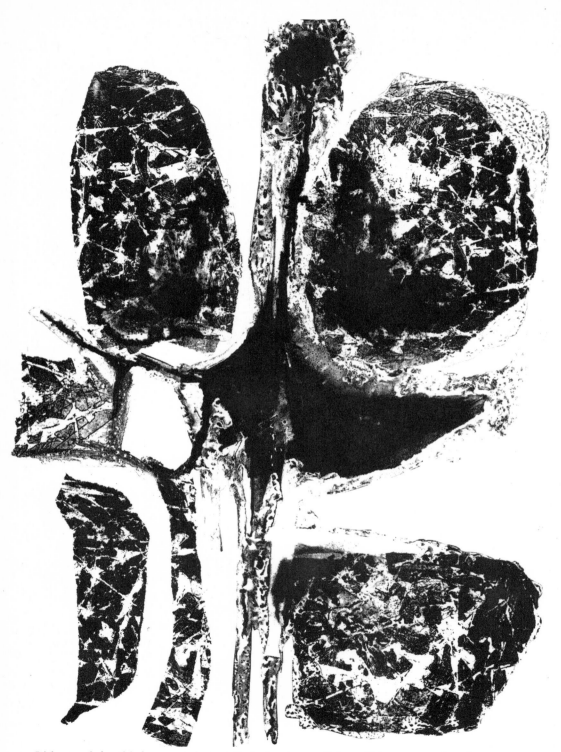

40 Lithograph by third year student at Bath Academy of Art. Prints were taken from
cut and incised hardboard; the prints were torn into shapes and printed-down on to
the lithographic plate. More work was added with litho drawing ink (tusche), both
full strength and diluted

41 *Morning Raga* 1964 by Henry Cliffe, lithograph, black, earth red and blue

42 Lithograph by third year student at Bath Academy of Art. Another example of wood grain printed on to a lithographic plate with other drawing added with ink (tusche)

43 Lithograph by John Hoskin 1962, drawn direct in chalk and ink. This lithograph is by a sculptor and shows concern with structure and form

44 *Foundry* by Sebastian Cliffe aged eleven—imaginative drawing direct on to plate

45 Lithograph by third year student at Bath Academy of Art. Print taken from wood plank; the printed plank transferred to lithographic plate by pressure. Further work was added with ink (tusche)

46 *Still Life with Spoon* 1955 by Jack Smith, drawn with ink, some diluted. The whites on glasses were taken out with caustic potash

47 *Still Life with Pears* 1955 by William Scott, drawn with ink, some diluted, printed in black over dark grey

will spoil both plate and lithograph, whereas if a colour is allowed to dry hard, any colour printed on top will show a tendency to shine. This is because the ink that has dried hard makes an impenetrable film which prevents succeeding colours from entering the absorbent texture of the paper; the ink thus remains on the surface and takes a long time to dry, resulting in a shiny print. This fault is very common when the inks used contain fairly large amounts of tinting medium, or when insufficient petroleum jelly has been added to the inks. Only experience will show how different inks react and how long they take to dry. Inks containing flake white, such as greys, pale blues or greens, will dry fairly quickly, as will chromes and oranges. Ink mixtures such as transparent blues, greens and pinks, take longer to dry. A good idea of the drying qualities of inks can be seen from the way that certain inks form a rubbery skin while still in the tin; these are the fast driers. There have been many more half-used tins of flake white wasted in lithography than there have been tins of press black.

Six or so trial prints have now been made and the plates have been altered and corrected. Experimental work has been done with different variations of the inks to be used and perhaps more work has been added to the plates or stones. A few more trial prints have finally been taken and show evidence of knowledge gained while printing them.

At this stage I clean my studio! It is as well to make sure that all table tops and working surfaces are quite clean and that no clutter, such as tins without lids or dirty palette knives, lies around the inking slabs. Most important of all, see that the inking slabs, rollers and press are really clean. The slightest film of black left on the inking slabs could turn a pale yellow into a lime green. Any pale colour can be ruined by dirty slabs or palette knives. A press is an efficient machine, but unless it is clean and in working order it soon becomes a mess and a bore. If you are using a lithographic stone as a bed for your metal plates, it should be clean with no little bits sticking to its surface. These would spoil the plate by denting it when the pressure is applied. Excess oil can ruin the paper or, much worse, get on the water or gum sponges and from thence on to the plate, resulting in a wasted plate.

When everything is to hand, cleaned up and in working order, printing the edition can begin.

The edition

An edition of prints means the number taken from a set of plates, and the smaller the edition the higher the price you may expect to get for each print. This is, of course, for the scarcity value and not for the quality of the print. The edition is, generally speaking, a limited one, and the normal number taken in lithography is fifty prints. In each case the artist retains a few prints extra to the edition.

These should be the first prints (proofs) taken; they are the artist's proofs and are usually limited in number to about six, or ten per cent of the total edition, and may command a higher price than the edition. This may not be sense, but it is common practice. (See *Definition of an original print*, page 93.)

First get out the sheets of paper required for the edition, either the total number of them, or perhaps twenty sheets for a start. Make sure that the paper is in a clean place and handy for the press. My own procedure is to print about four copies and then to hang them on the rack (see page 87). By doing this less table space is needed – a point to be considered when the studio is small. Of course if a friend will help it is ideal, because you can then concentrate on the printing while your assistant hangs up the prints with clean fingers.

In printing an edition one should make certain that every copy is as nearly as possible identical to the other copies in the edition. This means keeping a careful watch on the amount of ink that is carried on the roller, and how much is rolled on to the plate. Practice will soon make this second nature. Finally, the plate should be checked each time before a print is made, and also each print as it comes off the press, to make sure there is no dirt, spots or other undesirable things about that will spoil the work. This is important. I have many times seen cases where areas of the drawing have gradually filled in or disappeared as each successive print was pulled, and it was not noticed until too late. Looking at each print should become second nature – and a good print is always worth looking at for the sheer pleasure of it.

When the fifty of the first colour are printed and hung on the rack they are left to dry. When they are ready for the next colour they are taken down and stacked ready for printing as before, and then the second colour is printed. Again they are hung up and allowed to dry – the length of time will vary from the first colour, according to the drying capacity of the second one – and so on until the final colour is printed and the edition is complete.

The artist signs each print in the bottom right hand corner, clear of the printed image. On the bottom left hand corner of the printed image (this is important) put the number of the print starting at 1/50 (if fifty is the number of prints in the edition) and working through the edition to the last, which will, of course, be 50/50. An artist is usually allowed up to six proofs and on these 'Artist's proof' is written at the left hand corner with the number 1/6, 2/6 etc. beside it. It is also usual to add the year after the artist's name. Some printmakers insert the title of the print between the number and the signature, but it is not general practice.

12

Care of prints; exhibiting

Care of prints

Because of their fairly fragile nature, prints must be stored flat, in large stiff paper folders, in portfolios or in a plan chest (blueprint file) which will keep all the prints of one edition together.

Always make sure that you have clean fingers when handling prints; and do it carefully for there is nothing more depressing than torn or dog-eared prints. If finger-marks or dirt do, however, mark the borders of a print, use only a soft putty rubber (kneaded rubber eraser), or kneaded bread to remove them. Handmade printing paper has a fragile surface which if rubbed too hard will become fluffy and unpleasant and will ultimately look even worse than before the attempt at cleaning.

Prints should never be hung or stored in strong daylight because some inks used in printing may fade slightly.

Exhibiting

There are many opportunities for artist lithographers to show their work in the United Kingdom and the United States. Most mixed exhibitions will admit prints of one sort or another, and when one becomes expert enough there are galleries that deal exclusively with prints.

In Great Britain the Senefelder Club is an excellent body. It exists to further and exhibit the work of lithographers, and it holds exhibitions which travel around the country from gallery to gallery. The Print Council of America performs a similar function for all the graphic media. Usually prints must be submitted already mounted and framed.

If it is not possible to deliver the framed print by hand make sure that it is protected for its journey or it may well arrive damaged and with broken glass. Few galleries have either time or equipment to make good the damage.

If prints are delivered unmounted and unframed, then the simplest method of packing is to buy one or two stout cardboard cylinders large enough to take the prints. The best type have ends which can be removed and then all that is necessary is to roll the print, slide it into the cylinder and put tape round the ends, making sure that they are well secured. I need hardly emphasize the importance of addressing clearly and correctly the labels attached to the package.

When prints are sold through British galleries the dealer takes $33\frac{1}{3}\%$. If the dealer sells to another gallery for resale, both will take 25% commission. American dealers' commissions average $33\frac{1}{3}\%$ but may go as low as 25% or as high as 50%. Occasionally a dealer will buy the entire edition and the artist then receives about one-third of the nominal value of the lithographs, the dealer being responsible for all the unsold copies. Museums and other public bodies are usually given a discount when they buy, and this further reduces the amount payable to the artist. In America, the gallery usually absorbs the discount. Lithographs are usually sold unframed. A dealer will often be prepared to send copies of prints to exhibitions, sometimes even abroad.

There are many international print exhibitions, particularly in the United States, but the only way to exhibit at these is to write to the secretaries concerned, although artists are sometimes invited to send prints.

Addresses

The Senefelder Club is at $6\frac{1}{2}$ Suffolk Street, Pall Mall East, London, SW1.

Editions Alecto Ltd, 8 Holland Street, London, W8

There are Print Clubs in Philadelphia and other cities in the US. Information may also be obtained from the Pratt Graphic Art Center, 831 Broadway, New York 3, NY.

13

Equipment

Workbenches, etc.

The fittings and layout of a printing studio naturally depend upon the amount of space available.

It is essential to leave at least 3 *ft* all round the press; I believe that the conditions laid down for printing works make this a rule. It not only gives more room to move and work, but it helps to avoid any accidents. Every article or piece of movable equipment is best cleared away before printing, as a clear space is always needed to lay down a proof or check registration of colours.

Once the press is satisfactorily sited the question of bench space can be settled. Ideally a workbench of fairly heavy construction is needed to support the inking slabs. Inch thick planks are usually sufficient. The length and width of the bench naturally depend upon the space available in the studio, but the width should not be less than 2 *ft* 6 *in* and the length ought to be 6 *ft* or longer.

In my own studio there is a bench round three walls with cupboards underneath and racks for storing plates. The cupboards have shelves for storing a good number of prints. The plate racks have vertical divisions about 4 *in* apart; if the divisions are wider than 4 *in* the plates tend to buckle when stored in any number (figure 15.)

FIG 15 Work bench

For inking slabs I like to use lithographic stones which have been rubbed smooth, as the weight prevents them from sliding about. I use a slab about 2 *ft* × 1 *ft* 6 *in* for actually rolling up, and a smaller slab next to it for mixing the ink.

Roller racks

Next to the mixing slab should be a roller rack: two rollers are usually enough.

Figures 16 and 17 show the type of roller rack which I find most satisfactory. It is stout and simple in construction but has to be made specially for the purpose as it is not manufactured commercially. The rollers rest horizontally with the handles projecting so that they can be easily lifted out.

FIG 16 Roller and rack

Close to the roller rack there should be a space for sundries and bottles of chemicals. This is best made by dividing up an area of bench top into various sized boxes which can be done by nailing

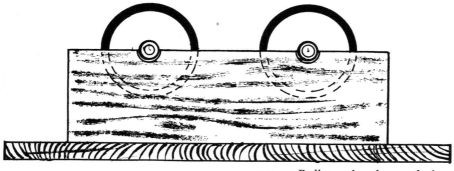

FIG 17 Roller and rack — end view

1½ *in* or 2 *in* doorstep slats on to the bench surface as shown in plate 26. One 'box' can then hold etch sticks, another chalks (crayons), another drawing ink (tusche), and so on. Everything is then to hand and there is no question of things being contaminated by their neighbours.

Always replace lids on ink tins and corks in bottles. A clean, tidy printing studio is efficient, but a dirty one can be both dangerous and costly.

Care of rollers

The litho rollers I use are made from a synthetic composition with an aluminium core and handles. They are light and easy to use, but because of their composition they are prone to damage from palette knives. Never scrape them or use a knife of any sort on them. Always keep them spotlessly clean with either paraffin (kerosene) or blanket wash, and make sure that there are no pieces of metal on the rags you use, such as buttons, hook fasteners or zippers. Anything of this kind can scratch and consequently ruin a roller, and rollers are expensive items of equipment. All this may sound obvious but it is surprising how often palette knives and rollers are left dirty.

Print rack

A rack for storing prints while drying is a useful piece of equipment in that it keeps clean prints away from working surfaces (see plate 25). It can be made on the same principle as a clothes airing rack, on a pulley fixed to the ceiling, or an ordinary wooden clothes rack can be adapted to hold the prints. On the wooden slats fix medium-sized bull-dog clips with screws. It is best to have the clips positioned so that each print is held by two clips, as this prevents the prints being twisted or distorted while drying; if prints are held by one clip only they have a tendency to curl, and this makes further printing difficult, apart from spoiling the finished appearance of the prints. Make sure that the clips you use are strong enough for the job, for if a heavy paper is being used there is a chance that it may slip to the floor. Also, with strong clips it is possible to conserve more space by hanging two prints back to back on one set of clips.

The siting of the rack is most important, especially in small studios and departments, owing to the necessity for hoisting the rack up to the ceiling or letting it down to clip on the prints. Free access must be given so that the ropes which support and hoist the racks up and down do not interfere with another working area such as a sink or bench. If it is necessary to stand at an angle to the rack when raising or lowering it, a lot of strain and heavy wear is imposed on the ropes, and I have seen a fully loaded rack come down when the rope snapped, simply because it was hung and used incorrectly.

A drying rack should not be sited above a radiator or any other form of heating as this makes the paper too dry for printing.

Fan

To make a fan for drying stones or plates, cut out a rectangle of stiffish card or strawboard about 10 $in \times$ 7 in. Cut two pieces of inch-wide tape, 4 in long, and fold them in half to make two flat loops. Stick or staple the ends of the loops on either side of one of the short edges of the card, about $1\frac{1}{2}$ in from the top and bottom; an 18 in length of $\frac{3}{8}$ in or $\frac{1}{2}$ in dowel rod is then inserted in the loops to form a handle. The finished fan looks like a small cardboard flag (figure 18), and by twirling it round and round over the plate or stone it can soon dry it completely.

It is possible to use a small electric hair-dryer in place of a fan.

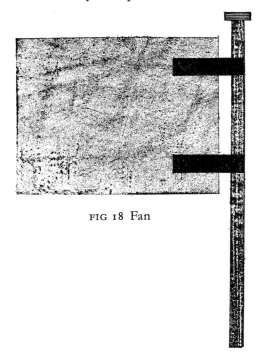

FIG 18 Fan

Lead weights

All that is needed is an old saucepan, some empty circular 1 *oz* tobacco tins and a small quantity of old lead piping or scrap lead. Melt the lead in the saucepan on a gas ring or stove and pour it into the empty tins. Usually it is sufficient to fill them two-thirds full. When the lead has cooled enough to enable the tins to be handled, replace the lids on the tins. This method produces clean and efficient weights. Old metal weights from scales are also suitable, of course, so long as they are perfectly smooth on the base.

Storage of stones

Stones will normally be stored in racks or on shelves below the workbenches. A small, sturdy trolley (dolley) is sometimes useful for moving them around from bench to sink or press.

Essential studio equipment

    Direct or offset printing press
    2 or 3 rollers
    1 roller rack
    1 stone slab for mixing ink
    1 stone slab for rolling up

Palette knives

1 or more working benches; part of the top sectioned for storing
 sundries

Cupboards and racks for storing plates or stones

Sink with running water

Hanging rack for drying prints

Fan

Lead weights

Dustbin (trash basket)

Jam jars and other containers for gum, etch, etc.

Teak stand for sink (if stones are used)

Trolley (dolley) (for moving stones)

Portfolios for storing prints

See also pages 26, 31 and 50 for materials such as inks, chemicals,
etc., used in drawing, processing and printing.

A simple frame

A frame can often be important for prints, and an attractive and
inexpensive one can be simply made. I would not, however, leave a
print in this type of frame for any length of time for, as will be seen,
it does not give complete protection against dust and damp.

The materials needed are all obtainable from most hardware shops
and lumber yards, and but a few tools are needed.

The basis of the frame is a piece of hardboard (masonite) 3 *in*
larger than the print on three sides and 4 *in* larger on the fourth side,
the bottom of the print. That is, in fact, the same size and proportions
as a normal mount which allows greater width below the print than
above; for if all margins were equal the print would appear to be
dropping out of the frame, and the wide lower margin corrects this
illusion.

It is advisable to make sure that the hardboard is a true rectangle
by checking with a set-square. Then lightly sandpaper the edges.
By its nature hardboard tends to be splintery stuff and if there are
any loose particles about they may end up between the print and the
glass.

When the hardboard has been sandpapered and the dust removed,
take a length of 1 *in* square wooden batten (strip) and mark off two
pieces exactly the same length as the long side of the hardboard.
Mark this accurately on all four sides of the batten with a carpenter's
square; this will make sawing easier. Saw off the piece of batten and,
using either hardboard pins (heavy brads) or impact adhesive, fasten
the wooden batten carefully to the rough side of the hardboard.
Always make sure that the edges are flush and the ends exactly in
line with the hardboard. Repeat this for the other long side of the
hardboard.

Measure off two pieces of wooden batten (strip) to fit exactly in the spaces on the two shorter sides of the hardboard (masonite), check the fit and make it glove tight. Fasten them in place. The work now resembles a shallow tray, but the batten still needs to be made firm at the corners. This can be done quite easily.

Make a hole with a bradawl (awl) or pricker through the side of each of the longer battens $\frac{1}{2}$ *in* from each end; carefully drive a 2 *in* oval nail through each of these four holes into the ends of the shorter battens. The tray should now be quite firm and rigid (figure 19).

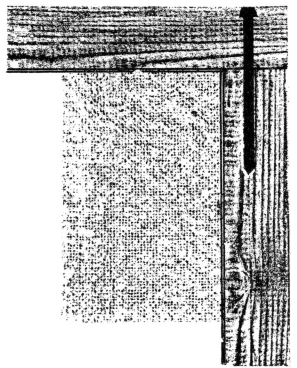

FIG 19 Worm's eye view of corner of frame

The shiny side of the tray should now be covered with a fabric sympathetic to the print; this may be either linen or rayon. I always use a fine, textured linen canvas, not too dark in tone. Lay the hard-board tray shiny side down on a piece of canvas and mark three inches beyond the edge all the way round. Bend the canvas over the edge in the centre of one side and drive a tack into the inside surface of the batten. Do the same on the opposite side, using some tension so that the canvas is stretched fairly tight. Do this on the other two sides, and then gradually tack the canvas down all round, working from the centre to the corners on each side. This method of working ensures that the canvas is stretched evenly, and that any surplus canvas ends up at the corners where it can be trimmed off.

The method of fixing the corners is simple. Cut out a square of canvas from each corner, then stick the remaining canvas down on the back of the tray with latex adhesive (rubber cement), so that the edges meet on the angle. This is mitring a corner.

The frame can be covered with paper instead of with linen and for this there is a much quicker and simpler method. Use a not too stiff paper and a good quantity of paperhanger's adhesive. Use the paste carefully so that it does not mark the paper and simply paste the paper to the shiny side of the hardboard, mitring the corners as with the canvas. Leave the paper a moment or two after it has been pasted before sticking it to the hardboard so as to give it time to stretch.

Unless you are proficient at cutting glass it is probably best to buy a piece from a paint or hardware shop (or a glass or picture frame shop in the US) exactly the same size as the frame; on no account must it be bigger, not even a fraction of an inch. Take an oil stone or sharpening stone and carefully rub down the edges of the glass. This is important because the frame will have no moulding and consequently, if the edges are sharp, fingers could be cut when handling the frame.

The glass must now be fastened to the front of the frame, and for this all that is needed are four right-angled clips to screw to the sides of the frame, holding the glass in place. These clips can be bought, but are expensive, and so I use the brass valance rail used for hanging pelmets (valances) over windows. This rail is about $\frac{3}{8}$ in wide and $\frac{1}{10}$ in thick. Cut with a hacksaw four pieces $1\frac{1}{2}$ in long; it is worth being accurate. Place the cut pieces in a metal vice with $\frac{1}{2}$ in showing above the vice, and with a hammer carefully bend the strip into a right angle (do not hit them too hard when bending or the brass may crack). When these four clips are made, place them again in the vice and bore a hole with a $\frac{3}{16}$ in drill, $\frac{1}{2}$ in from the end of the longer side. This will require patience and care but it is not difficult.

A final refinement is a small rubber pad – one cut out of an old inner tube of a motor tyre does very well. The pad should be as wide as the brass clip and $\frac{1}{2}$ in long. This pad ensures that when the clip is put in place no pressure is brought to bear directly on the glass by the metal clip; it acts as a shock absorber. The rubber should be stuck to the brass with 'Evostick' or a similar type of impact glue (contact cement) (figure 20.)

The final stage is to fix the glass accurately on the frame, the print fastened to the linen behind with strips of Scotch tape. Place a clip about 5 in in from the corner, on the bottom edge of the frame, and screw it into place with a $\frac{1}{2}$ in dome-headed No. 8 brass screw, or with wood screws. Screw the other three clips in place in the same way.

This type of frame is useful in a studio because it is a simple operation to change the print in the frame by merely unscrewing the clips. You may be able to think of variations or improvements to it which would make its construction even simpler.

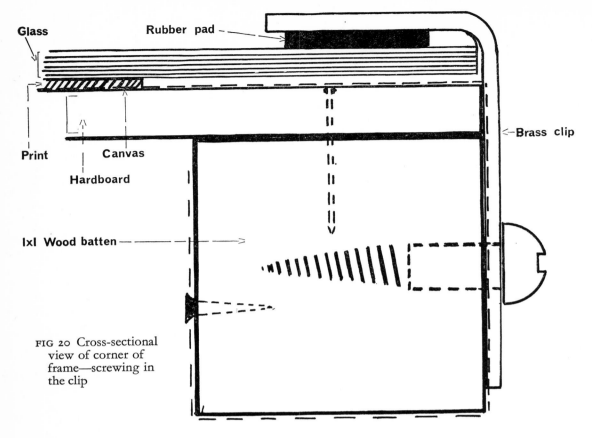

Glass **Rubber pad**

Print

Canvas

Hardboard

← **Brass clip**

1x1 Wood batten

FIG 20 Cross-sectional view of corner of frame—screwing in the clip

Materials and tools needed to make a frame

1 *in* square wooden batten (strip) (planed and prepared)

Fine-grained unprimed linen canvas or other suitable fabric, or medium stiff paper with a good texture

1 *ft* brass valance rail

Hardboard (masonite)

Hardboard pins (heavy brads)

2 *in* oval nails

1 tube of latex adhesive if fabric is used, or wallpaper paste for paper

1 $\frac{1}{2}$ *pt* tin of impact adhesive (contact cement)

4 $\frac{1}{2}$ *in* No. 8 brass dome-headed screws, or wood screws

Cellotape or Scotch tape

Tools

Set-square

Sandpaper

Carpenter's square

Hacksaw

Saw

Bradawl or pricker (awl)

Hammer

Oil stone

Metal vice

$\frac{3}{16}$ *in* drill

Screwdriver

The Definition of an Original Print was agreed at the Third International Congress of Artists, Vienna, 1960. In the following form it was produced by the United Kingdom National Committee of the International Association of Painters, Sculptors and Engravers (Association Internationale des Arts Plastiques, an affiliate of UNESCO) in 1963, after conferences with print-makers, publishers, art dealers and representatives of official bodies, and we are grateful to them for permission to reprint.

The Print Council of America (527 Madison Avenue, New York 22, N.Y.) have also produced a pamphlet, 'What is an Original Print?', which deals with editions, exhibiting, etc.

THE DEFINITION

1 It is the exclusive right of the artist-print-maker to fix the definitive number of each of his graphic works in the different techniques: engraving, lithography, etc.
See note (a)

2 Each print, in order to be considered an original, must bear not only the signature of the artist, but also an indication of the total edition and the serial number of the print. *See note* (b)
The artist may also indicate that he himself is the printer. *See note* (c)

3 Once the edition has been made, it is desirable that the original plate, stone, woodblock, or whatever material was used in pulling the print edition, should be defaced or should bear a distinctive mark indicating that the edition has been completed.

4 The above principles apply to graphic works which can be considered originals, that is to say to prints for which the artist made the original plate, cut the woodblock, worked on the stone or on any other material. Works which do not fulfil these conditions must be considered "reproductions". *See note* (d)

5 For reproductions no regulations are possible. However, it is desirable that reproductions should be acknowledged as such, and so distinguished beyond question from original graphic work. This is particularly so when reproductions are of such outstanding quality that the artist, wishing to acknowledge the work materially executed by the printer, feels justified in signing them. *See note* (e)

The following notes have been proposed by the United Kingdom National Committee as additional explanatory points and modifications of the Vienna definition.

(a) For the purposes of this definition, original prints may be classified in Great Britain as follows:

All prints pulled in black or in colours from one or more plates, stones, screens, wood blocks, lino blocks, etc., predominantly executed by the hand of the artist, either from his own design or *interpreting* the work of another artist or as a result of collaboration.

(b)
(i) Original prints may be produced in limited or unlimited editions. Limited editions are those in which the artist has decided to print a certain number only.

(ii) Prints pulled by the artist to show progress, called 'first state' or 'second state', etc., and artist's proofs, which are usually limited to about ten per cent of the total edition, should bear an indication to this effect and should not be included in the total number of this edition.

(iii) If the total edition is not indicated, the prints are liable to be treated as unlimited and therefore subject to purchase tax in this country or import duties abroad.

(c) The printer, if other than the artist, may add his name on the print.

(d) Prints which may *not* be classed as original prints are the following:

(i) Copies of original works of art made wholly by photo-mechanical or other mechanical processes even though they may be in limited editions and bear the signature of the artist whose work is reproduced.

(ii) Prints which may be described as a close or literal copy of an original work of art however produced.

(e) It is desirable that reproductions in this country be acknowledged and thus distinguished from original prints by printing on them the name of the artist, publisher and printer, even when the prints are signed or facsimile signed by the artist whose work is reproduced.

Appendix 2
List of firms supplying inks, paper and sundries

(Almost all these firms have overseas agents)

INKS

Lorrilleux and Bolton Ltd,
Eclipse Works, Ashley Road,
Tottenham, London, N.W.7

Manders Ltd,
2 Noel Street, London, W.1

J. H. and G. B. Siebold and
  Company Inc,
150 Varick Street,
New York, U.S.A.

Graphic Chemical and Ink Co
  Corporation,
728 N. Hall, Villa Park,
Illinois, U.S.A.
(also plates, paper, chemicals, etc.)

PAPERS

Barcham Green Ltd,
Hale Mill, Maidstone, Kent
(for Crisbrook, Bockingford and
imitation Japanese papers)

T. N. Lawrence & Son Ltd,
2 Bleeding Heart Yard,
Greville Street, Hatton Garden,
London, E.C.1
(for hand-made Japanese papers)

Andrew/Nelson/Whitehead Inc,
7 Laight Street,
New York 13, N.Y., U.S.A.
(for all print-making papers)

PLATES AND SUNDRIES

W. R. Nicholson Ltd,
58–62 Scrutton Street,
London, E.C.2
(plates, A Gum Z, rollers and
sundries)

Algraphy Ltd,
Willowbrook Grove,
London, S.E.15
(plates, A Gum Z, rollers and
sundries)

Hunter Penrose and Littlejohn Ltd,
109 Farringdon Road,
London, E.C.1
(plates, rollers, presses and
sundries)

Graphic Plate Graining Co,
246 Paterson Plank Road,
East Rutherford,
New Jersey, U.S.A.
(zinc plates)
(Plates may be returned to this
firm for regraining)

George Miller Co,
20 West 22nd Street,
New York, N.Y., U.S.A.
(all lithographic supplies)

NuArc Co,
4110 West Grand,
Chicago, Illinois, U.S.A.
(all lithographic supplies)

Rembrandt Graphic Arts Co Inc,
River Road, Stockton,
New Jersey, U.S.A.
(all lithographic supplies)

Craftools Inc,
Industrial Road, Woodbridge,
New Jersey, U.S.A.
(sundry supplies)

PRESSES

George Mann & Co Ltd,
Vickers House, Broadway,
London, S.W.1
(offset presses)

Kimber Ltd,
25 Field Street,
King's Cross, London, W.C.1
(reconditioned hand presses, inks,
stones and sundries)

PRESSES—*cont*.

Charles Brand,
84 East 10th Street,
New York 3, N.Y., U.S.A.

ROLLERS

Ideal Roller and Mfg. Co Inc.,
21–24 39th Avenue,
Long Island City, N.Y., U.S.A.

Index